Flying for Fun

How to take to the air

Keith Carey

Flying for Fun

How to take to the air
Keith Carey

 Patrick Stephens, Cambridge

First published in 1984

British Library Cataloguing in Publication Data
Carey, Keith
    Flying for fun.
    1. Aeroplanes—Piloting
    629.132'521   TL710
    ISBN 0-85059-705-6

Photoset in 9 pt and 10 on 11 pt Times by
Manuset Limited, Baldock, Herts. Printed in
Great Britain on 100 gsm Fineblade coated
cartridge, and bound, by The Garden City Press,
Letchworth, Herts, for the publishers, Patrick
Stephens Limited, Bar Hill, Cambridge,
CB3 8EL, England.

Contents

Acknowledgements

In common, I imagine, with most other authors, I find it difficult to know where to begin and end this section. The writing of this book was made possible with the help of a number of airminded people. I would like to express my thanks to the following individuals and organisations for their considerable cooperation and assistance: Gary Savage of Alan Mann Helicopters Ltd; Kenneth Simmonds of Thunder Balloons Ltd; M. Hurley of Flexiform Skysails; Malcolm Fath of Slingsby Aviation Ltd; Stan Abbott; British Gliding Association; British Balloon & Airship Club; H. Jeffrey of Norman Bailey Helicopters Ltd; A.R.B. Nash of Nash Aircraft Ltd; March Helicopters Ltd; David George of Sloane Helicopters Ltd; London School of Flying; CSE Aviation Ltd; Cameron Balloons Ltd; Colt Balloons Ltd; Amanda Bratt of Skyline Helicopters Ltd; Kaye Bradford of Westland Helicopters Ltd; Breen Aviation Ltd; British Hang Gliding Association; British Parachute Association; John Fuller of Weslake Air Services Ltd; British Aerospace Aircraft Group; Sue Lipsett of Airwave Gliders Ltd; Aero & Engineering Services Ltd; British Microlight Aircraft Association; Southern Sailplanes; Express Aviation Services Ltd; Headcorn Parachute Club; Tom Wright of Micro Biplane Aviation; and James Gilbert of Lemhurst Publications Ltd for permission to reproduce parts of David Ogilvy's *Flying Facts*.

Introduction

This book is a guide for the newcomer to the exciting world of aviation. It is not an authoritative manual of airborne training, but is intended to whet the appetite of the person who wishes to take up one of the sports described in these pages. I have not included items such as light aircraft or helicopter ownership as these are probably beyond the reach of the average would-be flyer. To the person interested in getting airborne at the weekend, the airspace above the United Kingdom appears hopelessly crowded. Air lanes, control zones and low level routes seem to fill the sky. The sort of flying we are interested in, however, mainly takes place well below these obstructions in what we call uncontrolled airspace.

In most parts of the country the amateur airman is left to pursue his sport without concerning himself too much with these technical complications. The sheer joy of flight on a summer's day is something that cannot be expressed in words. The earth when viewed from this new dimension unfolds into a strange and beautiful panorama. The shadow of the racing aircraft darts over woods and fields, toy cars seem to meander down the streets and lanes far below. The wings of your machine give a slight bump as a thermal of warm air rising from the fields below comes up to meet you in the sky. To the light aircraft or glider pilot, the parachutist or balloonist these and many other thrills are all part of being airborne.

Before you can experience these delights for yourself, you must undergo a strict training course in your chosen sport. This is essential so that you learn correctly and safely and do not endanger yourself or others. The various training programmes may seem strict and regimented, but the United Kingdom has an excellent safety record in airsports, and the individual controlling bodies and organisations are determined to keep it that way. To further assist the reader, a complete list of clubs and schools, useful addresses and a selection of books for further reading can be found in the reference section of this book. This should enable the would-be aviator to gain an understanding of his chosen sport without needing to question a busy club instructor item by item. One of the best ways to find out what will be required of you in your new activity is to take a trial lesson. This applies especially to potential light aircraft, helicopter, glider and balloon pilots. Now read on to see how you can become airborne.

Keith Carey
August 1983

Chapter 1

The light aircraft

First lessons

In this chapter we will take a detailed look at the training a potential student private pilot can expect to undergo and the further avenues of flying that will be open to him once qualified. The chief object of this chapter, therefore, will be to provide essential background information for the person attracted by the thought of taking to the air. No book or series of magazine articles can actually teach you to fly; only a qualified flying instructor imparting his knowledge to you in the aircraft cockpit can turn you into a pilot. The great majority of private flying in the UK is done in single-engined light monoplane aircraft such as the American Cessna 150 or Piper Cherokee 140 trainers. Both of these aircraft are ideal for the *ab initio* student to master the basics of airmanship. The Cessna 150 in particular is one of the world's best-selling light aircraft and is easy to fly, responsive and has no unpleasant handling characteristics. Thousands of these smart little two-place trainer/touring aircraft have left the Kansas production line of Cessna Aircraft.

People with no knowledge of flying often express surprise at the fact that light aircraft pilots do not wear parachutes. A parachute is no doubt an extremely useful item if your aircraft is being shot at by another aeroplane and is in imminent danger of plunging earthwards. Otherwise even a lightweight backpack is rather bulky in the small cockpit of a light aircraft and the chances of your Cessna being 'bounced' by a marauding Messerschmitt over the peaceful fields of southern England are nowadays rather remote.

A layman taking a quick glance into the cockpit of a modern light aeroplane may at first be bewildered by the seemingly complex array of dials, switches and instruments to be found there. A closer study, however, reveals that really they are not a lot different from those to be found in a motorcar. Apart from special instruments for flying such as an altimeter, magnetic compass, directional gyro, and artificial horizon, you will find a fuel gauge, rev. counter, speedometer, battery lever indicator and oil pressure gauge. As you can see, we are a long way from the complex instrument panels of modern jet airliners such as the Boeing 747 or McDonnell Douglas DC 10.

Opposite page
Top *The Piper Cherokee 140 light trainer.* **Centre** *Cessna 150 basic trainer.* **Bottom** *If you obtain a twin rating, you may then fly an aircraft such as this Piper Aztec.*

After reading everything on flying you can lay your hands on and after much careful thought and consideration you have decided to take up the challenge of learning to fly. After making contact with a club or school you duly arrive on the appointed day ready for your first lesson. You can wear what you would normally wear in your motorcar—the days of open cockpits and bracing wires humming in the wind are sadly gone for most of us, so sheepskin flying jackets, goggles and suchlike will not be needed. If you have not flown before, this lesson will serve as your air experience flight. It will either increase your desire to fly or send you home to shoot the cat. In the latter case you will have saved much wasted time and money. Even if you have flown before, this flight will enable you to become familiarised with the aircraft type on which you will subsequently train for your licence. Your instructor will first show you around the aeroplane in what is called the pre-flight inspection. You will not be expected to remember everything on this first lesson but you will notice that most of it is common sense. The tyres will be checked for correct pressure, the oil level checked and topped up as necessary, fuel filler cap securely fastened and so on. You may wonder why these items need to be checked at the start of every flight, but the pilot before you may have done something amiss, so it is sensible to satisfy yourself that all is well before taking to the air.

You will then get into the cockpit—you, the student, taking the left-hand seat and your instructor the right-hand seat. He will then start the engine and conduct a cockpit check pointing out to you some of the more important items. He will check the flying controls for freedom of movement and give you a brief idea of what each one does. After checking some vital actions and carrying out

The four forces acting upon an aircraft in flight.

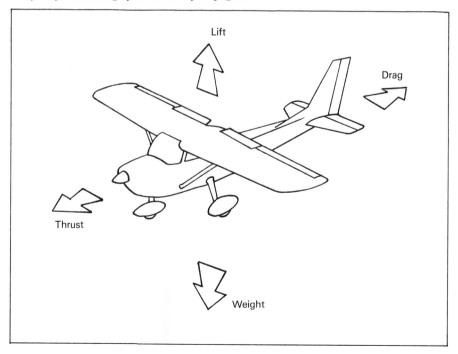

Above *The author about to take off on an instrument training flight in a Robin DR 400 aircraft.* **Below** *The author flying the Robin DR 400 on instruments. The plastic visor permits no vision outside the cockpit, thus forcing the pilot to fly by sole reference to the instruments.*

an engine run up check, he will obtain radio clearance, taxi out via the perimeter track to the active runway and take off.

Once away from the airfield the instructor will show you the effects of the various controls, keeping a sharp lookout for other aeroplanes, a habit you will be expected to adopt after your first few lessons. The instructor will ask you to look at the horizon ahead of you and, with you gently holding the control column, he will gently ease his forward and you will see that the nose of the aircraft goes down. He will then ease the control column gently back towards him and the nose of the aircraft will then come up. You will have noticed the small control movements involved, amounting to little more than gentle pressures—all in fact that is required.

Piper Dakota interior and instrument panel.

Next will come the sidewards movement of the control column. Look at each wing tip in turn and note that the aircraft is flying level. Then move the control column slightly to the left and you will see that the left wing goes down and the right wing comes up. Now ease the control column over to the right and the right wing will go down and the left wing will rise up. Return the control column to the central position and once again the aircraft will resume a level flying attitude. Lastly we have the rudder control. This produces the effect of yaw. Place your feet lightly on the pedals and apply a gentle pressure to the left pedal. You will see that the nose of the aircraft turns to the left, depress the right pedal and it turns to the right. These movements are called the primary effects of controls. The instructor will demonstrate all these exercises and then you will be asked to attempt them for yourself. As this is your first lesson, it will be a short one and apart from the manoeuvres already discussed you will not be expected to delve more deeply. The instructor will fly the aeroplane back to the airfield, join the circuit and land.

It should be stressed that although it is not unknown for a pupil to feel airsick during his early flights, it is usually overcome as the lessons progress. Many pilots never feel a qualm in the air but would not dream of boarding a cross channel ferry. As soon as this first lesson is over your instructor will start assessing your disposition for flying and building up your confidence in readiness for your first solo flight.

Before that can take place, however, there is much to be learned both on the ground and in the air. As your lessons progress you will receive theoretical classroom instruction in Meteorology, Navigation, Air Law and Aerodynamics, in preparation for when you are ready to sit for your written examinations. A requirement for your private pilot's training is that you must pass three written and one oral examinations in order to demonstrate that you have acquired sufficient theoretical knowledge. The pass mark for these examinations is 70 per cent and is usually taken at your flying club or school. For those student pilots who do not pass at the first attempt—and many fail one or other of the papers first time but pass with no problems on their second attempt—you will be able to retake the exams in particular subjects, but the complete examination must be passed within twelve months or the whole series of examinations will have to be retaken.

The written examinations

The ground examinations for the issue of a Private Pilot's Licence (group A) Aeroplanes are:

1 Aviation Law and Flight Rules and Procedures.

2 Navigation and Meteorology.

3 Aeroplanes and Principles of Flight.

4 Oral test on the specific aircraft type on which you are being tested.

A qualified military pilot serving in the armed forces is required to be examined in subject 1 and where applicable subject 4. The holder of a current flight navigator's licence is not required to pass subject 2.

Aviation law and flight rules and procedures

This examination is based upon a student's knowledge of the *United Kingdom Air Pilot*. The *Air Pilot* is a large book to be found at your flying school or club and contains everything you need to know regarding flight regulations and flying in the United Kingdom. Radio frequencies, navigation aids, airfields and

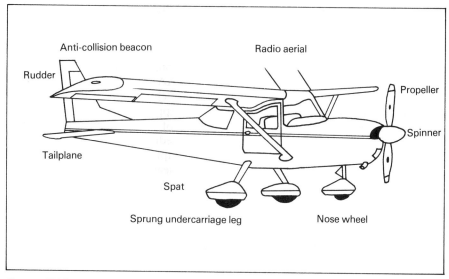

Cessna 150/152. Height 8 ft 7 in; length 23 ft 9 in; wingspan 33 ft 2 in; service ceiling 12,650 ft; oil capacity 6 quarts; fuel capacity 26 US gal; prop diameter 5 ft 9 in; engine Continental 0 200 A; speed 120 mph; gross weight 1,600 lb.

airspace regulations are just some of the topics to be found within its pages. The student pilot, however, is not expected to purchase his own copy of this expensive book. A smaller publication *Civil Air Publication CAP 85* will suffice for the student as it is based on extracts from the *Air Pilot*. The test paper on this subject may include questions on the following: types of airspace, airways and control zones, customs procedures, quadrantal and semi-circular flight rules, ground signals and aircraft lighting.

Navigation and meteorology

This is a very important paper, as presumably when you have your licence you will wish to fly across country. The ability to navigate accurately and safely is of prime importance. The Civil Aviation Authority views with absolutely no enthusiasm light aircraft and their pilots who stray into controlled airspace through faulty navigation.

Questions that may be included in this paper are locating and plotting positions, dead reckoning, compass variation and deviation, the 1 in 60 rule, types of cloud and the conditions required for their formation and the calculation of fuel consumption and ground speed. At a first glance this may seem to be a difficult paper, but the tuition your ground or flying instructor will give you will ensure that you enter the subject at the shallow end.

Aeroplanes and principles of flight

A general paper to test your knowledge on aerodynamics and aircraft systems.

Engines and airframes

This is the oral test in which the student pilot is required to demonstrate a general understanding of the group of aircraft he wishes to fly. The questions are of a general nature concerning engine performance and handling, oil quantities and levels, tyre pressures and sizes, carburettor icing and so on. The various requirements of the certificate of airworthiness may also be referred to.

By the end of the student's course of flying instruction questions such as these should pose no particular problems.

The flying test

The flying test for the issue of the United Kingdom Private Pilot's Licence will be conducted by a Civil Aviation Authority (CAA) approved examiner—most likely the chief flying instructor of your club or school—and takes approximately one hour to complete. The applicant will be required to demonstrate competence in the full sequence of flying manoeuvres and the correct observation of the relevant ground procedures. The rules of the flying test require that the student pilot under test occupies the left-hand cockpit seat of the aircraft and the examiner the right-hand seat. The flying test will follow the Civil Aviation Authority approved aeroplane syllabus.

Runways are referred to by their compass bearing in the direction of usage.

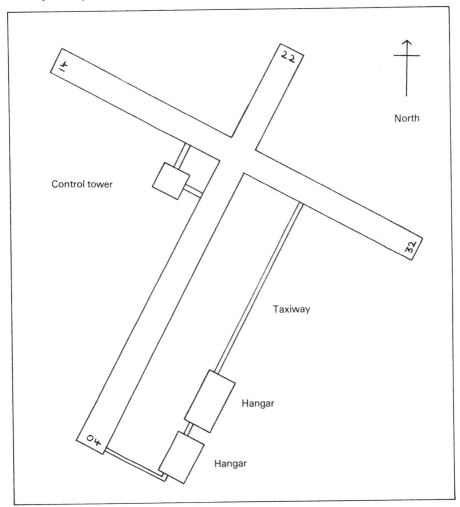

1983 model Piper Warrior II.

During the flying test the student pilot being examined will be assessed on airmanship, including circuit procedure, aerodrome discipline, the setting and use of the flight instruments fitted to the test aircraft, pre-flight inspection and engine start and run up procedure, cockpit check and vital actions. The test will usually consist of a flight lasting approximately one hour and will include the following:

1 Taxiing and take off, including the assessment of the cross wind component.

2 Engine failure after take off.

3 Action in the event of a fire.

4 Straight and level flight.

5 Short field landing (touchdown to be normally within 91 m [100 yds] of the edge of the landing area).

6 Assessment of landing with a cross wind component.

7 Landing the aircraft without power from a position and height selected by the test examiner.

8 Overshoot procedure from a powered approach.

9 Turns with various degrees of bank with and without engine power.

10 Climbing and descending turns.

11 Recognition of the approach to the stall.

12 Stalling and recovery.

13 Spinning and recovery (this will not be included in the test if the candidate can produce evidence, ie, from his/her logbook that he/she has safely recovered from a spin).

All pilots must complete these manoeuvres, but for those wishing to fly twin-engined aeroplanes (groups B and C) applicants must also demonstrate competence in the following:

1 The manoeuvres used in normal flight conditions with one engine shut down.

2 The approach and landing with one engine inoperative.

An applicant who fails any part of the test may be requested to undertake further dual flying instruction before being accepted for re-test.

Licence renewals

There are five different classes of air pilots. Private pilots are covered by groups A, B and C. The other two groups concern professional pilots such as air taxi, charter and airline pilots.

A private pilot's licence has to be presented to an instructor/examiner every 13 months and stamped to show that the pilot has met the experience level required. This means that you must fly a minimum of five hours as pilot in command (P1) every 13 months. If you do not fly as P1 for more than 25 months you must undergo further flight training and take another general flying test to renew your licence. The amount of experience required for the various groups is as follows:

Group A purpose	Flying single-engined aircraft under 12,500 lb for which the pilot is not remunerated.
Experience needed each 13-month period	Five hours pilot in command experience in an aircraft of the same group the pilot wishes to fly.
Group B purpose	Flying twin-engined aircraft under 12,500 lb for which the pilot is not remunerated.
Experience needed each 13-month period	Five hours pilot in command experience in an aircraft of the same group the pilot wishes to fly, including at least one flight in a twin-engined aircraft.
Group C purpose	Flying aircraft over 12,500 lb for which the pilot is not remunerated.
Experience needed	A Civil Aviation Authority technical type examination is required.

Medical requirements

Private pilots are not supermen and you only need hold a class three medical certificate issued by a Civil Aviation Authority authorised medical examiner. The typical charge for this examination is around £20 (1983) and your flying school or club can supply you with the names and addresses of local doctors authorised to carry out the examination. Your local GP cannot issue the certificate. You do not necessarily need to obtain a medical certificate before you start taking flying lessons, but it serves the dual purpose of being a student pilot's licence as well as a medical and you must have one before you will be allowed to fly solo. The medical examination itself it not unduly rigorous. It will include a general questionnaire on your health record and checks on hearing, reflexes, eyesight (no problem if you normally wear glasses or contact lenses provided your eyesight defects can be corrected to acceptable limits), respiratory system and blood pressure. Applicants over 40 years of age must also undergo

The Weslake W65/80-118-02 light aircraft engine. This new British engine is, at the time of writing, undergoing testing for installation in light aircraft and autogyros, offering 25-30 per cent lower fuel consumption than that of current light aircraft engines.

an electrocardiograph test and a chest X-ray. The certificate is valid for two years if you are under 40, for one year if you are over that age. There are some medical conditions which will usually exclude you from being granted a medical certificate. These include cardiac problems, diabetes that requires constant medication and epilepsy. So it is wise to complete your medical before starting flying lessons, thus saving both time and money if for any reason you should fail the examination.

Learning to fly

Now that you have completed your first lesson, you will start to learn the basics of flight, straight and level flying, turning, take offs and landings and general manoeuvring on the airfield. Also you should not make the mistake of thinking that your learning starts and finishes in the aircraft cockpit. It is possible to learn in this way but it will cost you far more in time and money in the long run. You should become familiar with the aeroplanes and the general activities on the airfield, so later on in your training you will find that you already possess a basic understanding of what is going on around you. Become familiar with the flight record sheet at your club or school so that you can see which aeroplane you will be flying and with which instructor as soon as you arrive. When in the flight briefing room, become acquainted with the various charts and information

The instrument panel of a modern light twin.

notices on the walls. Also, now that you are training to become a pilot you will
need a personal flying log book in which to enter details of your flights. This is a
legal requirement and you can obtain one from the office of your club or school
for a few pounds. Take care when filling in the various columns as you will find
it very satisfying to look back through the pages at a later date, recalling the
various flights.

The term 'airmanship' will be frequently used during your pilot training. It
covers all those parts of flying not directly concerned with the pure handling of
the aeroplane, such as not smoking in a hanger or in the vicinity of an
aeroplane, ensuring you can reach all the controls in the cockpit comfortably
and adjusting the seat and rudder pedals if necessary.

The basic course of flying instruction for the private pilot's licence is 43 hours
in length (38 hours for the approved course). Don't be alarmed at the term

Mooney Turbo 231 cruises at 220 mph at 24,000 ft.

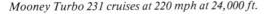

1980 model Piper Turbo Arrow.

'approved'. It does not mean in any way that the 43-hour courses are inferior, but that to qualify for the shorter syllabus you must complete your course of lessons within six months, whereas the unapproved courses let you spread your training over as long a period as you wish. The course is divided between dual and solo flying. The student will fly approximately 20 hours dual and 23 hours solo.

During the first part of your flying training, say up to the first 12 hours, the instructor will be continually assessing the pupil pilot in readiness for his first solo flight. The timing of this event by the instructor is of prime importance. If the student is allowed to fly solo before he is ready, the resulting flight could be an unnerving and dangerous affair. If it is left too late, the student may lose interest in flying, with the resulting deterioration in his personal flying standard. The student who progresses satisfactorily will be permitted to fly solo after about eight or nine hours and it will be the most important moment of his/her flying training, if not airborne career. Many people would imagine that this moment, when the instructor leaves the aircraft and the pupil pilot is on his own must be a worry or dread. Most students however look forward to it and think they are ready to fly solo long before their instructor considers them competent to do so. A student being sent on his first solo is despatched quickly without being given time to worry over it, the instructor telling him to go through his checks and then making some nonchalant remark like, 'you know what to do so off you go.'

The first solo is unique and you will have experienced something that can never happen again throughout your life. You will be expected to perform a normal take off, fly a circuit of the airfield and land. You will also be required to cope with any emergency that may arise during the flight. It must be said that while there may be the occasional bad landing, there are rarely bad accidents during first solos. The first solo flight does not in any case mean the end of dual flying with your instructor, there is plenty more of that to come during the next few hours of the course. This period will involve consolidation exercises, circuit flying and the approach and landing including some hours of solo flying again on the decision of the flying instructor.

As a point of interest the check list for the Cessna 150 aircraft is as follows:

Pre-starting checks

Parking brake On.
Controls Check all controls full and free movement ailerons, rudder, elevator, etc.
Fuel cock Check set in 'on' position.
Mixture Set to fully rich.
Throttle Set quarter inch open.
Carb heat Full and free movement set to cold.
Radio Off.
Electrics Off.
Primer Prime as necessary.
Master switch On.
Magnetos Both on.

After starting checks

RPM Set at 1,000.
Oil pressure Green.
Magnetos Check both for drop.
Radio On.
Electrics As required.
Flaps Up.
Instruments Check all instruments.
Gauges Check temperatures and pressures.

Taxiing checks

Check brakes. Check compass and directional gyro in both left and right turns.

During the remaining hours of the course, as well as consolidation exercises and more circuit work, there will be some advanced exercises away from the aerodrome, where you will undertake some turns that are more ambitious than those covered in the pre-solo stage. These steep turns will help to improve your coordination and confidence in handling the aircraft. Also included in this period of advanced training will be stalling and spinning. You may ask why you will be taught stalling and spinning, especially if you are only interested in flying

1981 model Piper Seneca II.

straight and level. The answer is that both stalling and spinning are the results of misusing the aeroplane's controls, so it is important for you to learn the following:

1 How to recognise an approaching stall, ie, low airspeed, control response;

2 How to recover quickly and efficiently with the minimum loss of height;

3 How to recover from a spin should you enter one as a result of bad handling at or near the stall.

Forced landings with and without power will also be covered giving the student pilot experience in selecting emergency landing grounds such as stubble fields, heathland and beaches etc. Also included in your training will be four hours' training in instrument appreciation work intended to give you an insight into instrument flying skills and problems.

By now you will have passed your written and oral examinations and your flying training will have been concentrating on increasing the practical application of what you have learned so far.

Preparation for the Licence

At this stage in your pilot's training you will have a period in the air with your instructor in which you will go over all the exercises that you have learnt so far. You will probably go through each sequence of your syllabus once or twice to check that you have it absolutely taped. If both you and your instructor are satisfied that you are ready to have a crack at the General Flying Test for the Private Pilot's Licence you will find yourself with an appointment with an authorised examiner, most likely the chief flying instructor of your own aero club or school. The manoeuvres you will be required to perform during your flying test have already been detailed.

1982 model Piper Seminole.

Above left *The author's Private Pilot's Licence.* **Above right** *The author's Radio-Telephony Operator's Licence.*

The examiner is not there to fail you or trip you up, his aim is simply to assess whether or not you are ready to exercise the privileges that go with the granting of the Private Pilot's Licence and in making the decision he carries a certain heavy responsibility. Once you have qualified for the licence you may fly a British registered aeroplane, so long as it has only one engine and weighs under 12,500 lb, anywhere in the world. The same privileges apply to a twin-engined aircraft should you later take a course in twin flying and qualify for a group B rating. The examiner will expect a little more polish than your instructor did when sending you off on your first solo, but will also be interested in your airmanship and general handling. You would almost certainly be asked to attend a re-test if you taxi carelessly, fail to carry out your checks, disobey radio instructions or indulge in any other malpractice. But he will probably excuse, say, a slightly untidy approach and landing as long as you know what you did wrong.

If all goes well and you have submitted your formal application, only a week or so will elapse before you hold your licence. This will permit you to take your friends and relations on joyriding flights, demonstrating your new skill and sharing with them the joy of seeing the geometrical patchwork of the British countryside from the air.

Private pilot ratings

As his knowledge and flying experience increases the private pilot may wish to obtain the following ratings.

Radio telephone rating During training it is permitted for a student to use aircraft radios without a licence. When qualified, however, a licence is required by law. The R/T licence is gained by a written paper and practical test.

Night rating A night rating will enable the holder of a private pilot's licence to fly as pilot in command at night in an aeroplane in which any passenger is carried.

Instrument meteorological conditions rating This is useful both from a practical and safety point of view. It is designed to give the pilot the capability to fly in conditions below the basic PPL minima.

Instrument rating This qualification permits the holder to fly in controlled airspace, on airways and in bad weather. There is a written examination to pass and a stringent flying test with a CAA examiner from the Civil Aviation Authority Flying Unit.

Twin rating A twin rating will enable the pilot to fly twin-engined aeroplanes. A flying test and oral examination will need to be passed.

Seaplane rating This will enable the holder to fly float planes and amphibious aircraft from lakes, rivers and open water, etc.

Instructor rating An assistant flying instructor or full instructor's rating will enable the holder of the licence to give instruction in flying aeroplanes of such types that may be included in the rating.

Jet aircraft A jet aircraft will require an individual type rating on your private pilot's licence before you can fly them. They are very rarely flown by private pilots and only by you if you happen to own an oilwell.

How much will it cost?

The crunch. As with most things, it comes down to money at the end of the day. Learning to fly is not cheap, only less expensive than some other sports. For around the cost of a good second-hand motor car or summer holiday in the eastern Mediterranean, you could become the holder of a private pilot's licence. The prices at flying clubs and schools vary a great deal and although you should aim to learn at the club nearest to your home, it does pay to shop around. Make a list of clubs in your area and visit them in turn before parting with any money. When you arrive at the club of your choice, does anyone bother to ask if they can help you? If your reception is offhand then try somewhere else. Remember, you will be spending the best part of two thousand pounds on gaining your private pilot's licence and if that particular flying club or school does not seem to want your business, then there are plenty more elsewhere that do.

Other good pointers to an efficient and friendly club or school are: How many aeroplanes do they have available for training? Are they kept clean? Are there separate briefing rooms for the ground school instruction? Are the premises clean and tidy? Are the staff attentive? How many instructors do they have? And so on. There is no difference between a school or club, usually it is only the name. But at some of the smaller clubs you may find yourself being roped in for tasks such as answering the telephone, making coffee, getting aircraft out of hangers etc. These small outfits frequently operate on a members self-help basis and are usually friendly and efficient clubs.

At the time of writing (1983), the average hourly rate at flying clubs and schools is around £30 to £45, so it would be wise to budget for around £1,500 to £2,000 for the private pilot's licence course.

Should money for your training be a problem a number of clubs and schools offer finance facilities negotiated with popular finance companies. Most clubs and schools also take credit cards such as Access or Barclaycard. A personal loan through your bank manager may be another way of finding the cost of training.

Now take a look at the price table below; it gives a cost breakdown at a typical club or school.

The Average Aero Club Ltd

Club membership fee	£40
Medical examination fee	£20
Hire of Cessna aircraft for 20 hours dual at £39.50 per hour	£790
Hire of Cessna aircraft for 23 hours solo at £32.00 per hour	£736
CAA Licence issue fee	£77
Total	£1,663

To this total can be added the cost of various textbooks, navigation computers, protractor, rulers, maps and pilot log book.

After obtaining your PPL

Obviously you will be proud of yourself and of your shiny new pilot's licence. It is an extremely worthwhile qualification to have and there are only about 20,000 holders in the United Kingdom (population over 53 million). Now that you are a pilot, by all means spread your wings and make the most of your new licence. Regardless of whether you fly for pleasure or business, remember you have only 40-50 hours of flying experience and are still very much a learner. There is an old saying in light aviation which is very true, 'The issue of a private pilot's licence is just a licence to learn.' So, no matter how apt a pilot you are, or think you are, stay within your limits until you have built up more practical flying experience. The most obvious obstacle in the United Kingdom is our often foul and dirty weather. Even the most experienced professional pilots can be caught out by mother nature. If you are planning a cross country flight, watch the television weather reports and also get a proper meteorological forecast and if during the flight you encounter conditions beyond your experience TURN BACK.

Failure to turn back in deteriorating weather conditions is one of the biggest causes of general aviation accidents in the world. It is nicknamed 'press on itis' and it is a killer. There is no shame in turning an aeroplane around because of fog or heavy rain. It comes under the heading of good airmanship which we outlined earlier; it is also called COMMON SENSE.

Let us now examine some of the dos and don'ts for the private pilot. First a private pilot may not fly for 'hire or reward'! This means the pilot may not receive any remuneration for flying. To fly for reward one must qualify for one of the professional licences such as a CPL or ATPL. Second, if the pilot takes a fancy to overfly his local football team on a Saturday afternoon he will be breaking civil air law. An aeroplane must not fly over or within 915 m (3,000 ft) of any open air assembly of more than 1,000 people. This rule will be waived if written permission from the event organisers and the Civil Aviation Authority has been obtained.

Private flying is one of the safest ways in which to travel, on average much safer than the family motorcar. If you keep to flying in reasonable weather, thoroughly prepare your flight plan, make sure you have enough fuel plus

Above *When you obtain your PPL, it will also qualify you to fly self-launching motor gliders, such as this Brasov IS 28M2 A.* **Below** *The instrument panel and cockpit layout of the Brasov IS 28M2 A.*

reserves for the intended journey and apply plenty of common sense, you will not go far wrong. Remember, flight in cloud or bad weather requires instrument flying skills and as a newly-qualified private pilot you will not possess them.

Now that you are a fully fledged pilot, however, you will be able to hire aircraft for touring purposes if you so wish. There are a number of companies offering self-fly hire arrangements and prices vary a great deal from outfit to outfit depending on how long the aircraft is hired for. Many pilots soon build up a list of favourite trips and places such as Paris and Amsterdam are within two hours flying time, Biarritz and Frankfurt within three. One of the most popular trips for a private pilot with a few hours' experience under his belt is to fly across the English Channel. The very sound of Le Touquet for the weekend presents many attractions and nowadays few problems. All the pilot has to do is present his passengers and himself at a customs equipped airport for personal clearance. He will then have to sign a form giving a written undertaking that the aeroplane will return to the United Kingdom within a month. If the aircraft should land at an airfield that is not customs equipped, he must obtain their consent before the aeroplane unloads or leaves the area. The pilot will then be free to cross to one of the Channel Islands or to mainland France.

Aerobatics

It is necessary for a brief description of aerobatics to be made in this chapter. Many pilots, once they have been flying for a while, like to acquire new skills. For those not interested in taking courses in radio navigation or continental touring, aerobatics offer a whole new freedom of the sky.

In the past, when flying clubs and schools were equipped with Tiger Moths or other aircraft types suitable for aerobatics, relatively few private pilots wished to take up the art. Now that these machines have been replaced by monoplane trainers and touring aircraft, more and more pilots are being introduced to the art. Still, there is a feeling among private pilots that aerobatics are for experts or people who have been fortunate enough to have been trained in the armed services. The basic manoeuvres, however, are within the reach and capability of many pilots if they are prepared to work at the training in a realistic and organised manner. Before attempting any of the approved aerobatics, each of the following should be considered to ensure that the flight will be safe and enjoyable.

Take some dual aerobatic flying instruction No aerobatic manoeuvres should ever be attempted without first having received dual instruction from a qualified aerobatic instructor. This applies to all pilots, but especially newly-qualified private pilots.

Physical condition The pilot should be in good physical condition and mentally alert. Initial aerobatic flights should be limited to a maximum of 30-45 minutes so that the pilot can become gradually accustomed to the unusual flight attitudes typical of this type of flying.

Seat belts and harnesses Seat belts and harnesses should be adjusted to provide proper restraint during all flight conditions. Care should be taken, however, to ensure that the pilot can easily reach all the flying controls.

Loose equipment The cabin should be clean and all loose equipment should be securely fastened. For solo aerobatic flying the co-pilot's seat belt and harness should be secured.

There are several simple and basic rules to remember when performing aerobatics. You must always be well away from any controlled airspace, be over open country, away from cloud and at a safe height. A safe height means being at least 915 m (3,000 ft) above ground level. In case anything should go wrong, this will give you enough height to put things right. You should also carry out clearing turns in both directions to ensure all is clear and find yourself a conspicuous landmark to use as a reference point for when you have completed your manoeuvre. Before you start to learn aerobatics you must be a smooth flier. This does not mean you have to be a pilot of 'Red Arrows' calibre, but your flying and handling of the aircraft's controls should be balanced and well coordinated. Apart from this all you need to be is an average club trained private pilot. Aerobatics are not for everyone, but if the idea of a slow roll, loop or barrel roll on a calm summer's evening appeals to you, then go ahead. Aerobatics are there for all to enjoy, even you.

H	Height	Sufficient to recover with plenty of spare. Normally not less than 915 m (3,000 ft) for stalling or aerobatics or 1,525 m (5,000 ft) for spinning, but depending on local rules.
A	Airframe	Brakes, undercarriage, flaps, canopies etc, as appropriate to type. DI caged for spinning or aerobatics.
S	Security	Hood, hatches and harness. No loose articles in cockpit.
E	Engine	Mixture rich, pitch, carburettor heat. Engine instruments oil pressure, temperature.
L	Location	Clear of controlled airspace. Prominent landmark in sight.
L	Lookout	Clear of cloud and other aircraft. To be checked by clearing turns.

Below *The spin.* **Above right** *The loop.*

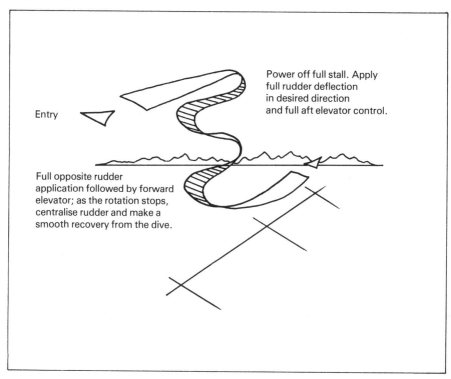

Power off full stall. Apply full rudder deflection in desired direction and full aft elevator control.

Entry

Full opposite rudder application followed by forward elevator; as the rotation stops, centralise rudder and make a smooth recovery from the dive.

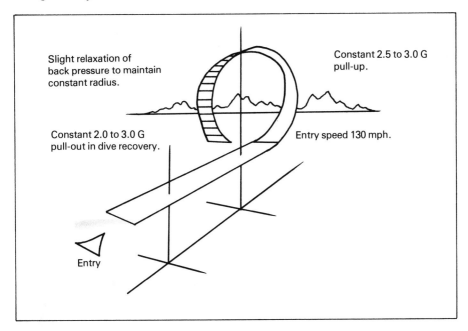

Slight relaxation of back pressure to maintain constant radius.

Constant 2.5 to 3.0 G pull-up.

Constant 2.0 to 3.0 G pull-out in dive recovery.

Entry speed 130 mph.

Entry

Nash Petrel specifications

The Nash Petrel aircraft is a rugged, metal aircraft with a powerful engine and good handling qualities. Petrel has a proven glider towing performance. It has an excellent rate of climb and very effective flaps, ideal for small field operations. Visibility from the bubble canopy is outstanding, important for flying training and glider towing. The Petrel is easily deriggable and can be transported by road.

The cockpit

Entry is via a backwards sliding canopy. The layout inside has been carefully designed. There are two throttles, one on the left of the cockpit and one on the central console. Dual controls use sticks and seat positions are adjustable. Fuel controls and gauges are grouped together so that functions and readings are unambiguous.

Undercarriage

The undercarriage is a long wheelbase, no-maintenance tricycle with steel leaf spring main legs and a telescopic nose leg. The nose wheel is steered directly from the rudder pedals to give positive steering while taxiing. There are hydraulic disc brakes on the main wheels operated by a hand brake lever.

Engine

The Petrel prototype has been flown with 180 and 160 hp Lycoming engines. Production aircraft can be fitted with engines from 118 to 180 hp.

Span   29 ft 4 in
Wing area   136 sq ft
Length   20 ft 5 in
Height   7 ft 4 in
Empty weight   1,190 lb
Take off weight   1,680 lb

Fuel capacity   23 imp gal
Cruising speed   105 kt
Stalling speed clean   45 kt
Stalling speed full flap   40 kt
Rate of climb   1,100 ft per min

Above *Nash Petrel aircraft under construction at Farnham, Hants.* **Below** *A new British-designed and -built aircraft, the Nash Petrel.*

Exercise numbers used in flying training

1 Familiarisation with the aircraft.
1E Emergency drills.
2 Preparation for flight and action after flight.
3 Air experience.
4 Effects of controls.
5 Taxiing.
6 Straight and level flight.
7 Climbing.
8 Descending.
9 Turning.
10 Stalling.
11 Spinning.
12 Take off and climb to downwind position including engine failure after take off.
13 Approach and landing including overshoot.
14 First solo.
Consolidation exercise:
(a) Glide approach and landing.
(b) Engine assisted approach and landing.
(c) Short take off and landing.
(d) Cross wind take off and landing.
(e) Flapless landing (if applicable to type).

(f) Wheel landing (if applicable to type).
(g) Sideslipping (if applicable to type).
(h) Stalling.
(i) Spinning.
15 Advanced turning.
16 Operation at minimum level.
17a Forced landings without power.
17b Forced landings with power (precautionary).
18a Map reading and compass headings.
18b Dual cross country no 1.
18c Dual cross country no 2.
18d Solo cross country no 1.
18e Dual cross country no 3.
18f Solo cross country no 2.
18g Dual cross country no 4.
18h Solo cross country no 3 (test).
Instrument appreciation.
Revision for final test.
GFT General Flying Test.
19 Instrument flying.
20 Night flying.
21 Aerobatics.
22 Formation flying.
23 Asymmetric flight.

Above *A student pilot and instructor take to the air in a turbine-engined Bell 206 Jetranger.* **Below** *The Enstrom 280 Shark.*

Chapter 2

Flying a rotary wing

To those who love flying, the ability of the modern helicopter to hover and fly in any direction, be it forwards, sidewards or backwards, under complete control, gives a unique thrill and fascination that is not found in any other branch of powered flying. Also, from the passengers' point of view, the lack of speed during the lift off or landing gives a feeling of safety to those unused to flight. The practical helicopter is a relatively new aircraft on the aviation scene, although its design in its earliest form can be traced back to the fifteenth century, when Leonardo Da Vinci sketched a spiral wing which he theorised would bore its way through the air. Da Vinci's ideas were sound enough, but the lack of engine power retarded rotary wing development for hundreds of years. Various helicopter designs appeared in the early part of this century, but the VS-300 machine of Igor Ivanovitch Sikorsky, a Russian from Kiev, is acknowledged as the forerunner of present-day helicopters.

Throughout history man has dreamed of duplicating the flight of birds. In the rotary wing approach to the fulfillment of this, the first important development occurred late in the 15th century when Leonardo Da Vinci sketched a spiral wing which he theorised would bore its way through an air mass.

Above *A Hughes 300 light helicopter.* **Below** *An increasingly popular aircraft for* ab initio *rotary wing training is the Robinson R22, pictured here at the Westland Heliport on the River Thames.*

Whilst flying a rotary wing aircraft is one of the most exhilarating forms of powered flying available, it is also one of the most expensive. For purely fun flying where its operating costs cannot be offset against business or commercial use, it is only flown by the fortunate few. However, should helicopter flying appeal to you and fall within your budget, there are a number of schools offering tuition up to private pilot's licence standard. These schools are mainly concentrated in the southern part of the United Kingdom and are far fewer in number than their fixed wing counterparts.

Most prolific among light piston engined helicopter trainers are the following

three models Bell 47, Enstrom F28 and 280 Shark and Hughes 300. The Bell 47 is the oldest design of the machines currently available for training. The design of this helicopter goes back to 1943 and it first flew on December 8 1945. The first type approved certificate and the first commercial licence were awarded to the Bell 47 on March 8 1946. It was also built under licence by Westland Helicopters in England and by Augusta in Italy. It went out of production with the parent company Bell Helicopters in 1974, thus ending 28 years of continuous production. It will be familiar to most people from the American television series *M.A.S.H.* and *Whirlybirds*. The Enstrom and the Hughes are both three-place light trainers of American design. The Enstrom first flew in May 1962 and the Hughes 300 in October 1956. The Hughes 300 is also a well proven trainer for military pilots. Designated the TH-55A, it has trained over 30,000 pilots for the US Army alone, clocking up more than three million hours' flying time. All three of these aircraft are excellent introductions for the student new to flying rotary wing aeroplanes.

It is a common misconception that it takes a virtual superman to fly a chopper. Tales of helicopters being notoriously tricky to fly have been largely promulgated by other, self-aggrandising helicopter pilots. It is more demanding to fly, especially for an *ab-initio* student, than a fixed-wing aeroplane, but should present no undue problems for a student of average ability. The Civil Aviation Authority has approved a training syllabus for the student helicopter pilot in line with those laid down for fixed-wing aeroplane operations.

The instrument console of the Robinson R22 helicopter.

The following pattern is laid down for the General Flying Test.

1 Pre flight inspection.
2 Engine starting procedure and running up.
3 Air taxiing.
4 Take off, hovering and landing into wind.
5 Flying a square pattern with constant heading of speeds not exceeding 25 knots.
6 Take off, turn 360 degrees each way in hovering flight, perform a cross wind landing within the limitations of the helicopter type.
7 Straight and level flight at pre-determined airspeeds and power settings.
8 Climbing and descending turns.
9 Steep turns at constant altitude and airspeed.
10 Entry into autorotation and overshoot procedure.
11 A landing in simulated autorotation in a selected area.
12 In a servo assisted helicopter, an approach and landing using the supplementary system.
13 Recognition and correction of 'over pitching'.
14 Limited power take off and landing.
15 Action in the event of a fire.
16 Flight into and out of a restricted landing area.
17 Aircraft shut down procedure.

Bell 47 G-4 check list

As a point of interest the check list for the Bell 47 G-4 helicopter is as follows:

Before starting

1 Blade untied.
2 Controls, friction off/freedom of movement.
3 Collective full down.
4 Cyclic centred.
5 Mixture off.
6 Carburettor heat cold.
7 Battery and generator off.
8 Starting vibrator normal.
9 Magnetos off.
10 Instruments static position.
11 Altimeter set.
12 Engine/transmission oil temperature engaged.
13 Hydraulics on.
14 Lights off.
15 Breakers in.
16 Ag-breakers out.

Starting

1 Mixture auto or full rich.
2 Battery on.
3 Magnetos on both.
4 Throttle prime and set.
5 Clear.
6 Starter depress.
7 Engine rpm 1800.
8 Engine oil pressure check.
9 At 150 rotor rpm slightly roll back throttle to join needles.
10 Throttle advance to 2,300 rpm.
11 Generator on (note loadmeter).
12 Controls:
(a) Check tip path plane.
(b) Check freedom.
13 Engine oil temperature check in green.
14 Cylinder head temperature—check in green.
15 Throttle 3,200 rpm.
16 Check magnetos—max 200 rpm—50 rpm difference.
17 Freewheeling unit—check split needles.
18 Magneto safety check (turn off and on quick).
19 3,200 rpm friction as desired.
Instruments green.

During your flying training all these manoeuvres will be well covered by your flying instructor. He will also teach you how to perform maximum performance take offs, slope landings and running or high altitude take offs and landings. The two flight terms that probably need further explanation are autorotations and high altitude take offs.

Autorotation

If the engine of your helicopter should fail in flight you may think the aircraft will drop like a stone, but as a fixed-wing aeroplane has its wings to glide with, so a helicopter has its rotor blades. Autorotation, therefore, is a non-powered flight condition in which the helicopter will descend with its rotor system being

Many of the civil Bell 47s now flying started life as military machines such as this Sioux in Army markings.

driven by the action of the relative wind only. A controlled descent can be made because the individual rotor blades are still producing lift. The pilot is thus able to select a moderate or steep glide angle depending on the available landing site. In an autorotational descent the air enters the rotor system from below rather than from above as in powered flight.

High altitude or running take-off and landing

Running take-offs or landings are used when sufficient power is not available for a vertical take-off/landing because of a heavy load and or high density altitude conditions. Even a helicopter equipped with a skid undercarriage can be slid along the ground utilising translational lift until flying speed is reached (see figure below).

Limited power or running take-off. **1** *Holding available power, the cyclic stick is eased forward and the helicopter is slid along the ground.* **2** *When the helicopter feels light on the skids, ease back the cyclic stick and fly a few inches off the ground.* **3** *Keep building airspeed using translational lift.* **4-7** *Keep building airspeed.* **8** *Now you have sufficient airspeed, climb away.*

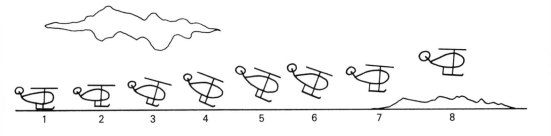

The written examinations

The subjects for the written examinations for the issue of the Private Pilot's Licence Helicopters/Gyroplanes are as follows:

    1 Aviation Law and Flight Rules and Procedures.

    2 Navigation and Meteorology.

There are also two oral examinations to be passed:

    1 Rotorcraft (general).

    2 Engines and Airframes (specific type).

Helicopter flight theory and aerodynamics are more complex for the rotary wing student than those of his light aircraft counterpart. A thorough knowledge will be required of subjects such as disc loading, blade coning, gyroscopic precession, hunting, blade stall, advancing blade, solidity ratio, torque, translational lift, rigid rotors and transverse flow effect. As for the private pilot's licence (aeroplane) written examination, a pass mark of 70 per cent is required. The holder of a current flight navigator's licence is not required to pass written examination number two. For those student pilots who do not pass at the first attempt, you will be able to re-take particular examination subjects, but the complete examination must be passed within twelve months or the whole series of examinations will have to be re-taken. The privileges of the private pilot's licence (helicopters/gyroplanes) are:

    1 The holder of the licence shall be entitled to fly as pilot in command or co-pilot of a helicopter or gyroplane of any of the types specified in the aircraft rating included on the licence provided that:

    2 He does not fly a helicopter or gyroplane for the purpose of public transport or aerial work.

    3 He shall not receive any payment in respect of the flight other than payment for the giving of instruction in a helicopter or gyroplane owned or operated under arrangements entered into by a flying school of which the person giving and the person receiving instruction are members.

    4 He will not act as pilot in command (PIC) on a night flight on which passengers are carried unless his/her licence includes a valid night rating.

An Enstrom Shark of the south coast distributor, Spoonair. The small wheels on the skids are to assist with handling the helicopter while on the ground.

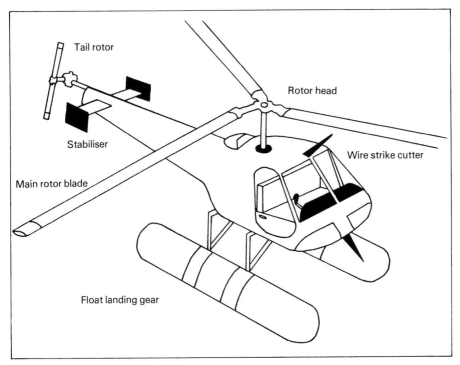

Enstrom F28 light helicopter. Height 9 ft; length 29 ft 4 in; main rotor diameter 32 ft; max operating altitude 10,000 ft; cruising speed 100 mph; max baggage 60 lb.

Medical requirements

The medical requirements for the private helicopter pilot's licence are identical to those for the light aircraft pilot. You need only hold a class three medical certificate issued by a Civil Aviation Authority authorised medical examiner. The typical charge for this examination is around £20 (1983) and your flying school can supply you with the names and addresses of local doctors authorised to carry out the examination. Your local general practitioner cannot issue the certificate. You do not necessarily need to obtain your medical certificate before you start taking flying lessons, but it serves the dual purpose of being a student pilot's licence as well as a medical and you must have one before you will be allowed to fly solo. The medical examination itself is not unduly rigorous. It will include a general questionnaire on your health record and checks on your hearing, reflexes, eyesight (no problem if you normally wear glasses or contact lenses provided your eyesight defects can be corrected to within acceptable limits), respiratory system and blood pressure. Applicants over 40 years of age must also undergo an electrocardiograph test and a chest X-ray. The medical certificate itself is valid for two years if you are under 40, for one year if over that age. There are some medical conditions which will usually exclude you from being granted a medical certificate. These include cardiac problems, diabetes that requires constant medication and epilepsy, so it is wise to complete your medical before starting flying lessons, thus saving both time and money if for any reason you should fail the examination.

Ratings

As his knowledge and flying experience increases the helicopter pilot may wish to obtain the following ratings:

Radio-telephony rating During training it is permitted for a student to use aircraft radios without a licence. When qualified, however, a licence to operate airborne radios is required by law. The R/T licence is gained by a written paper and practical test.

Instructor rating (helicopters) An assistant flying instructors rating (helicopters) will enable the holder of the licence to give instruction in flying helicopters of such types that may be included in the rating.

Turbine conversion type rating This is necessary when converting from a piston-engined machine on to a turbine-powered aircraft. A pilot converting from the Bell 47 to the Bell jet ranger will generally need at least five hours of dual instruction. With the hourly rate at approximately £225, this will cost around £1,121 (1983). Once type rated, the jet ranger will allow a greater freedom of operation for the pilot. Its gas turbine engine is controlled automatically, instead of by the twist grip throttle. It will offer superior speed and performance in all aspects of the flight envelope.

Night rating This will entitle the holder of the private pilot's licence (helicopter/gyroplanes) to act as pilot in command at night of a helicopter or gyroplane in which any passenger is being carried.

Piloting the helicopter

What is it like to learn to fly one of these marvellous machines which have been described by both pilots and engineers alike as a 'collection of spare parts flying in loose formation'? The initial difficulties in learning to fly a helicopter are usually due to the lack of coordination when operating the various controls. Unlike a fixed-wing aeroplane, where if you get into difficulties you can take

Right *The cabin layout of the Gazelle with the cyclic and collective controls clearly visible.*

Below left *The most striking external feature of the Gazelle is the ducted-fan tail rotor. Called a 'Fenestron', it is part of the secret which enables the machine to cruise at nearly 170 mph.*

your hands off the controls and the aeroplane will sort itself out, a helicopter is not inherently stable and good coordination is a skill that can only be acquired through practice. Is the helicopter easy to fly, therefore? The answer to this question is not straightforward. A student pilot may initially have more difficulty learning to fly a rotary wing aircraft than his/her counterpart student learning to fly a light aeroplane. When the flying course is completed, however, helicopter handling may be easier because of the simpler take off and landing techniques, range of speed available and better cockpit visibility. The helicopter pilot will certainly be more fatigued after a few hours' flying, than an aeroplane pilot conducting similar work. When flying a rotary wing aircraft, the pilot seems to be doing very little, his hands barely moving. In fact the pilot is making constant small corrections with the controls, maintaining position with the cyclic pitch stick, keeping the correct height with the collective pitch lever, adjusting the anti-torque (rudder) pedals and feeding in small inputs of rpm.

Basic helicopter controls consist of the following:

Cyclic stick (steering control) Equivalent to the elevator and aileron control stick in a fixed-wing aircraft. Controls directional movement of the aircraft, forwards, backwards, sideways and left and right turns while in forward flight.

Anti-torque pedals Equivalent to the rudder pedals of a fixed-wing aeroplane. These control the increase or decrease of pitch on the tail rotor. Used to keep aircraft on a heading parallel to the desired line of flight. Also used for spot turns and precision work while in the hover. Any change in collective pitch or throttle will require a compensating change in pedal pressure.

Collective pitch lever (up and down stick) No equivalent in fixed-wing aeroplanes, it is so named because it increases and decreases the pitch of the

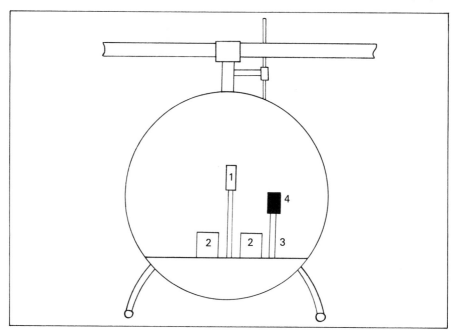

Controls of the helicopter and their principal functions. 1 Cyclic control stick—controls attitude and direction of flight. 2 Anti-torque pedals—maintain heading. 3 Collective pitch stick—controls altitude. 4 Throttle—controls rpm.

rotor blades collectively. It bears some similarity to propeller pitch control. Controls take off, climb and descent of helicopter.

Throttle (piston engine) Equivalent to fixed-wing aeroplane throttle. Twist grip throttle mounted on and synchronised with the collective pitch stick. The throttle can be adjusted independently of the 'collective control' and is used independently in engine starting, warm up and other rpm adjustments required while in flight.

Throttle (gas turbine engine) When the helicopter is powered by a gas turbine engine, the normal control of the power unit by twist grip throttle is changed to automatic control. The twist grip is often retained, however, as an emergency manual throttle or rpm select control.

Trim control Equivalent to a fixed-wing aeroplane trim control. Used for compensating control pressures caused by variable in flight conditions.

Friction locks Equivalent to the friction nuts on a fixed-wing aeroplane. Used to adjust hand pressures of controls to individual requirements, plus positive locking of controls in any position.

Rotor brake No equivalent in fixed-wing aeroplanes. Provides smooth and gradual engagement of the main rotor system.

Engine off landings, hovering on the spot and transitions from the hover to forward flight and vice versa are the main aspects of initial helicopter training. The more advanced manoeuvres such as advanced autorotations, out of wind manoeuvres and flight into the vortex ring condition follow later on. The exercise which seems to present most difficulty to student pilots is hovering. The

The turbine-engined Bell 206 Jetranger.

ability to hover a helicopter motionless over a fixed spot is the single most important skill a potential rotary wing pilot has to master. This is important so that the helicopter can be landed smoothly. Any sidewards movement could tip the machine over and backwards movement might cause the tail rotor to strike the ground. Let's take a look at lifting a helicopter from the ground into a hover and transitioning into forward flight.

A vertical take off is a manoeuvre in which the helicopter is raised vertically from a spot on the ground to the normal hovering altitude (1 m/3 ft as measured from the bottom of the skids or wheels to the ground) with a minimum of lateral and/or fore and aft movement. The helicopter should be faced into wind prior to engine starting. Using the throttle, set hover rpm with the collective pitch lever in the full down position and the cyclic control stick in the central or neutral position. Apply left anti-torque (rudder) pedal for torque compensation. Now smoothly raise the collective pitch lever and adjust the throttle to maintain the proper rpm. (Throttle adjustments should be made by means of a 'slow squeezing movement'—it is often said 'just think of the adjustment and that's enough' and indeed it is often so.) As the helicopter becomes light on its undercarriage, make necessary cyclic adjustments to ensure a level attitude on becoming airborne. When the skids or wheels leave the ground adjust the collective pitch setting smoothly to effect a hover at approximately three feet of altitude. Now, while in the hover, a clearing turn should be made prior to departure from the hovering area. Then smoothly and slowly ease the cyclic control forward from the neutral position to build airspeed and follow immediately by raising the collective pitch lever to prevent settling when the helicopter departs from its ground effect. A lesser amount of left anti-torque (rudder) pedal will now be needed to maintain a straight flight path over the ground. As forward speed is obtained, continue to increase the collective pitch control. Adjust the cyclic control as necessary to gain about one foot of altitude per mile of airspeed. In the transition from hover, to climbing forward flight the helicopter will be in a nose down attitude. As the helicopter continues to climb forward and as the airspeed reaches climbing speed, raise the nose of the aircraft to the climbing attitude. The normal climb attitude is approximately the same as that of the helicopter when standing on level ground. The helicopter will fly in this attitude until the desired height is reached. As airspeed increases, the use of left anti-torque (rudder) pedal is decreased. A straight flight path over the ground is of the greatest importance and cannot be over emphasised.

When flying helicopters one is instructed never to do anything suddenly or violently, just gentle manoeuvres. Hovering in ground effect probably accounts for most of the training time, learning to coordinate all four controls. All sorts of little dance exercises are devised, such as the moving of the tips of the skids around the four sides of a square at a height of a foot or so, flying in a circle while always facing the centre or always facing outward, or flying a square halting the helicopter at each corner, then turning 90 degrees at a time while hovering motionless. It's amazing how much fun one can have and how much challenge one can find flying a helicopter within a foot of the ground within 30 m (100 ft) of the lift off point.

Once it is up in the air and flying along, a helicopter does not behave all that differently from a fixed-wing aeroplane. You do not need anti-torque (rudder) pedal in turns, but other handling is similar, ease the stick forward the chopper speeds up and descends, ease back and it slows and climbs, ease to the side and it banks and turns. What's different of course in the rotary wing is the transition from hover to forward flight and back again. Lift offs to the hover and forward flight we have already discussed. Landings however are trickier at first, especially if you are a fixed-wing pilot converting to helicopters. Such pilots have a hard time bringing themselves to accept the fact that they can terminate the landing approach by flaring all the way to a standstill without stalling and crashing. An aeroplane-style circuit is flown with downwind, base and final legs and the idea is to pick the intended landing place through the cockpit canopy, freeze it in position and watch it grow as you approach at a constant descent angle. Ideally, as your airspeed decreases steadily and constantly, power must be increased since the helicopter is getting part of its lift from its forward speed through the air. It is a skill that only comes through practice and you may spend several fruitless hours, flying the same approach again and again, possibly terminating by getting too slow, too far out or speeding too fast helplessly past the touch down point.

As the approaches fall into place, however, you will soon move on to explore some of the more advanced manoeuvres. Steep approaches, 'quick stops' (in which the helicopter is rapidly decelerated from a forward airspeed of 45 mph or so), roof top landings and flight in the vortex ring condition. The flight condition known as 'vortex ring' can occur during a vertical descent with power on, a descent rate in excess of 90 m (300 ft) per minute usually being necessary. In the case of this vertical descent, the effect can be prolonged with partial loss of control and vibration depending on the type of helicopter being flown. Therefore, steep or vertical approaches to touch down points in calm air should be carried out at a low rate of descent to avoid encountering the condition. The

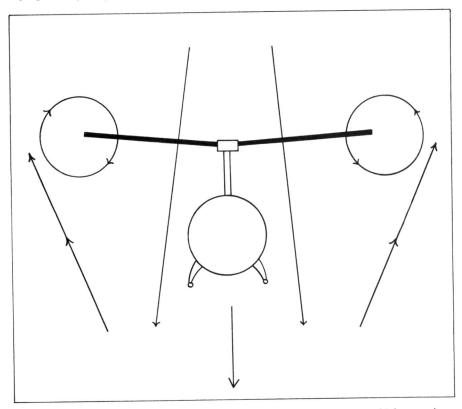

The airflow pattern of a helicopter in the 'vortex ring', a condition which sometimes occurs during powered vertical descents.

'vortex ring' is so called because of the airflow pattern around the main rotor (see figure above). If the condition is met with, there are two methods of recovery:

1 Ease the cyclic stick forward and dive out of it.

2 When entering autorotation, bottom the collective pitch lever and dive out of it.

Once these manoeuvres are learnt, the remaining part of the course becomes much more fun. Low flying, dashing across fields, hopping over hedges, night flying and confined areas, landing the helicopter in a small clearing bounded by trees and telegraph wires, the dust and leaves scattering under the swirling downwash of the rotor. By now there only remain a few areas to be brushed up on before the 1179 general flight test. Landing on soft ground, slope landings and a final refresher on autorotations. Then, on successful completion of the test you, the holder of a private pilot's licence (helicopter/gyroplane), will be entitled to fly a helicopter for personal pleasure or business use. When the helicopter student first qualifies for his licence, he/she will not be permitted to fly out of sight of the ground or water until he/she has passed a course of basic instrument instruction—usually five hours with an instructor will enable him/her to gain the endorsement.

Brantly Hynes Model B2 pilot check list

Pre-starting

1 Adjust seats.
2 Fasten seat belts.
3 Fuel valve on.
4 Rotor brake on (pull up).
5 Wheel brake on (wheel gear).
6 Mixture lean (out).
7 All switches off (radio, lights etc).

8 Check controls for freedom.
9 Collective down.
10 Throttle closed.
11 Magneto key to both.
12 Master switch on.
13 Generator switch on.

Starting hot

Proceed directly to step 5 on cold start procedure.

Starting cold

1 Mixture full rich (in).
2 Fuel pump to on/auto pressure checked.
3 Open throttle until indication of fuel flow, then close.
4 Turn fuel pump off.
5 Set throttle for starting (listen for clicks).
6 All personnel clear of aircraft (clear rotor).
7 Cyclic control neutral.

8 Start engine idle 1,000 rpm.
9 Rotor brake off (down).
10 Watch for oil pressure rise.
11 Join engine and rotor tach needles (clutch engagement should occur within 20 seconds).
12 Idle 1,700/2,000 rpm until engine and oil temps in green.
13 Lights, radios on as required.

Run up

1 Increase rpm to 2,000, check freewheeling clutch (split needles).
2 Check engine transmission temperature.
3 Set altimeter to field elevation.
4 Secure doors, re-check seat belts (both seats).
5 Increase rpm to 2,900/3,200, check magnetos.
6 Check engine driven fuel pump pressure in green.

7 Turn electric fuel pump on, leave on in flight.
8 Check wind direction and speed.
9 Check instruments in green.
10 Release wheel brake (wheel gear).
11 Start to lift collective, check blade track and stick position for proper loading.

Post-flight

1 Make walk round inspection, look for any signs of damage.
2 Log flight time, make note of fuel remaining.
3 All switches off, rotor brake on.

Brantly helicopters at a flying school prepare for another busy day's training.

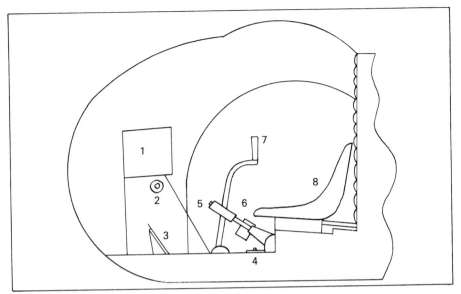

Above *The cabin layout of a Brantly B2.* **1** *Instrument console.* **2** *Instrument light dimmer.* **3** *Directional control pedals.* **4** *Nose trimmer.* **5** *Throttle/collective pitch control.* **6** *Starter switch.* **7** *Cyclic pitch control stick.* **8** *Pilot's seat.*

Below *Brantly Hynes Model B2 pilot preflight checklist.* **1** *Park helicopter into wind away from congested area.* **2** *Put wheels 'up', locking pins in place, handling bar in helicopter.* **3** *Determine fuel quantity and flight requirements.* **4** *Check oil level, normally 4.5 to 5 quarts.* **5** *Check generator belt for tightness.* **6** *Check engine compartment for oil leaks and general condition.* **7** *Secure cowling.* **8** *Check cockpit, switches off, rotor brake off.* **9** *Turn rotor backwards at least 30° to check clutch.* **10** *Check outboard blades for parting of bonding, cracks, etc.* **11** *Check swash plate for side play, remove dirt and grit from area.* **12** *Check all control linkages for freedom and lock nuts.* **13** *Check oil cooler belts for tightness.* **14** *Check oil cooler area for cleanliness.* **15** *Check landing gear fittings at fuselage and skids for cracks.* **16** *Check tail rotor drive shaft.* **17** *Check fuselage skin for damage or wrinkles.* **18** *Check tail rotor pylon for damage or wrinkles.* **19** *Check tail rotor area, pitch links, bell crank, push rod, etc.* **20** *Check tail rotor oil level.* **21** *Check tail rotor guard.* **22** *Check tail rotor blades.* **23** *Drain fuel sumps, two locations.* **24** *Check baggage secure, door closed and locked.*

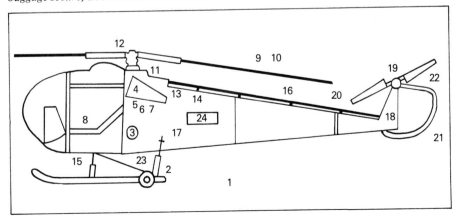

A Brantly B2 equipped with floats touches down on a lake.

Helicopter exercise numbers (Norman Bailey Helicopters Ltd)

1 Familiarisation with helicopter.
2 Preparation for flight/action after flight.
3 Air experience.
4 Effects of controls.
5 Power and attitude changes—level flight—turns.
6 Climbing and descending—including turns.
7 Autorotations.
8 Hovering.
9 Take offs and landings.
10 Transitions.
11 Circuits and emergencies.
12 First solo.
13 Sideways and backwards flight.
14 Spot turns.
15 Vortex ring.
16 Engine off landings.
17 Advanced autorotations.
18 Forced landings.
19 Steep turns.
20 Precision transitions.
21 Quick stops.
22 Pilot navigation.
23 Out of wind manoeuvres.
24 Sloping ground.
25 Limited power.
26 Confined areas.
27 Instrument flying.
28 Night flying.

In order to pass your flight test and remain a good helicopter pilot you should be able to demonstrate and discuss the following:

1 The flight manual of the helicopter you fly.
2 Normal flight in a smooth and predictable manner.
3 Slope landings and take offs.
4 Loss of tail rotor landings.
5 Familiarity with your helicopter's sounds and vibrations.
6 Engine failure in the hover.
7 Normal, shallow and steep approaches.
8 Limiting factors on speed and how to detect stalls.
9 Height velocity chart.
10 Recognition of and correction of 'over pitching'.
11 Vertical take offs.
12 Flight into and out of a restricted landing area.

Remember, to be professional in your flying, a thorough pre-flight inspection as outlined in the helicopter flight manual is the first step to a safe and enjoyable flight.

How much will it cost?

As we have said, helicopter flying is not cheap. Its expense can be attributed to the following three factors:

1 Higher and more frequent maintenance costs than fixed-wing aircraft.

2 Higher insurance premiums.

3 Higher salaries commanded by helicopter instructors, often ex military pilots.

Today you can expect to pay around £5,000 for your private pilot's licence (helicopters/gyroplanes). A typical helicopter flight school is that of Norman Bailey Helicopters Ltd of Southampton (Eastleigh) Airport in Hampshire. This school is authorised by the Civil Aviation Authority to conduct helicopter pilot training for the issue of the private pilot's licence (helicopter). They are also approved for courses of instruction for the assistant flying instructor's rating (helicopter), type conversion training, flight tests 1179(H), night ratings and basic instrument flying. The standard of instruction can be assessed from the fact that this school carries out training with officers of the Civil Aviation Authority and conducts training contracts on behalf of overseas governments.

The approved course of instruction for the private pilot's licence (helicopter) consists of 35 hours of flying time (30 in the case of the holder of a current

The Bell 206 Longranger is a seven-seat helicopter developed from the five-seat Jetranger II. Clearly visible on the skids are the 'pop out' floats which enable the machine to land on water in an emergency.

aeroplane licence undergoing helicopter conversion). This school can offer courses on a full-time basis, in which case the necessary flying can usually be completed in about three weeks according to the student's aptitude and the weather conditions. Alternatively, the training can be arranged on an ad-hoc basis to suit the mutual convenience of the student and the school. Flying training at this school is normally carried out in the Hughes 300 helicopter which is also the standard trainer for the US Army. Basic instruction can also be carried out on turbine powered aircraft such as the Hughes 500 or Bell 206 Jetranger by prior arrangement. The price of turbine training, however, will be considerably more expensive than that of the piston engined Hughes 300. The 1983 cost of training courses with Norman Bailey Helicopters Ltd on the Hughes 300 are:

1 CAA approved 30 hour course for fixed-wing pilots converting to helicopter including the required ground school subjects: £4,250 plus VAT.

2 CAA approved 35 hour course for ab-initio students together with all necessary ground schooling: £4,900 plus VAT.

These prices also include all the necessary textbooks, study guides, maps, scales, protractors and pilot log books etc.

If a full-time course is taken or a block of flying hours are purchased some training schools may be prepared to negotiate a reduction in the hourly flying rate. Most basic helicopter flying training is given in single rotor, piston engined aircraft such as the Bell 47, Hughes 300, Robinson R22 or Enstrom F28 or 280. Should the trainee pilot wish, gas turbine powered helicopters such as the Hughes 500, Westland Gazelle or Bell 206 Jetranger are available for basic flight training or type rating. If a helicopter student trains for his licence exclusively on one of these turbine powered aircraft, the overall cost of his/her flying training will be much higher than that of the standard piston engined course. The average hourly cost of a turbine powered helicopter such as the Jetranger works out at approximately £225 per flying hour dual and £207 per flying hour solo. The following table gives a breakdown of turbine training costs.

School membership fee	£40
Medical examination	£20
Turbine helicopter flying 20 hours dual at £224.25 per flying hour	£4,485
Turbine helicopter flying 15 hours solo at £207.00 per flying hour	£3,105
CAA licence issue fee	£77
Total	£7,727

Operating restrictions

Once the helicopter pilot has qualified for his licence, the countryside becomes a playground for his highly versatile machine. He does not need any runways or aerodromes on which to take off or land and is free to operate from farmers' fields and private property as long as it is done within safety limitations and permission of the landowner has been obtained. Office to office, factory to factory, building site to building site or any other combination you can think of, the helicopter is quick and flexible. The ease and pleasure of speeding over congestion and delays below means arriving at your destination with a confident

A Gazelle flying over London.

flourish. This is definitely what helicopters are all about. Using a helicopter saves valuable time that would otherwise be spent on the road incurring the weariness of long-distance travel. Helicopters offer quick point-to-point travel as shown by these typical journey timings, courtesy of Norman Bailey Helicopters Ltd:

From Southampton to
Exeter—55 min
Bristol—35 min
Cardiff—50 min
Birmingham—1 hour
London—40 min

From Rainham (East London) to
Dover—35 min
Felixstowe—40 min
Norwich—50 min
Southampton—45 min
Hull—90 min

Helicopters can also fly to out of the way places, such as setting down on a small island or sandbar in the middle of a fast flowing river, the swirling water only a few yards from the skids. These and other adventures are unique to the helicopter and cannot be found in any other branch of flying. When operating over towns, cities or other built-up areas certain rules must be applied. Aviation law requires that the helicopter pilot must not fly below such a height that would enable it to land safely without risk to persons or property in the event of an engine failure and subsequent autorotation. A helicopter must not fly below a height of 457 m (1,500 ft) above the highest fixed object within 610 m (2,000 ft) of the aircraft without first obtaining official permission. Certain parts of the city of London are forbidden to helicopter traffic. There are, however, special lanes set out for the use of helicopters, and it is not by chance that the River Thames is the main thoroughfare for helicopter traffic. The surface of the river

A French-built and -registered SA 341 Gazelle.

and the adjoining land above the high tide mark present a natural emergency landing ground in the event of a forced touchdown. There are also two heliports operational on the River Thames; one being the Westland helipad at Battersea and the other being a converted barge moored at Trig lane in the shadow of St Paul's Cathedral.

Most pleasure flying, however, will take place well away from these obstructions and if you operate from land or water, for which special flotation gear is available, you will be flying one of the most unique aeroplanes yet invented. Flying a chopper is as much fun as anything you can do in daylight with people watching and if you should get lost, you can always slow down to walking pace and read the roadsigns.

Westland-Aerospatiale Gazelle (civil version)

The Westland-Aérospatiale Gazelle is a five-seat light-weight general purpose helicopter ideally suitable as an executive or freight transport. Forming part of the Anglo-French helicopter cooperation programme, the Gazelle is under construction for the military and civil markets in both England and France. Powered by a Turbomeca Astazou three gas turbine the Gazelle offers transportation with the comfort of a limousine combined with speed. The unobstructed cabin interior gives easy access and panoramic views. Within a matter of minutes the Gazelle can be changed from a passenger to freight transport vehicle. The seats fold away to provide 2.27 m³ of cargo space complete with tie down rings. With an all-up weight of 1,700 kg and empty weight of 883 kg, the Gazelle has a maximum speed of 310 km/h and can transport 660 kg of freight over 680 km. Overall length (rotors turning)—11.94 m; overall width (rotors turning)—10.50 m; overall height (rotors turning)—3.16 m.

Chapter 3

Gliding

All gliding that takes place in this country, and indeed most other countries, takes place at club level. A glider, unlike a powered aeroplane, cannot launch itself without assistance from others. This is why a gliding club is a good place to make new friends—new members are always welcome. There is always plenty of work to be done on the ground at the gliding field, driving the tow car, operating the winch, getting gliders out of the hangar or helping with putting them away, acting as signalman and various other launch point duties. At this level, club gliding is one of the least expensive and most enjoyable, if time consuming, ways of becoming involved in sporting aviation.

The first man-carrying glider in this country was built by an Englishman, Sir George Cayley, and flown by his reluctant coachman across a small valley on his estate at Brampton, near Scarborough in Yorkshire in 1853. The triplane that Cayley built, had all the ingredients of a flyable aircraft, all that was needed was a powerful lightweight engine to make possible the progress from gliding to powered flight. Unfortunately the most efficient powerplant available throughout the nineteenth century was the too heavy steam engine. Another aviation pioneer, Percy Pilcher, a marine engineer, made many successful gliding flights near Glasgow in Scotland and later at Eynsford in Kent from 1895 to 1899. But these were simple gliding flights on a descending course. The present popularity of gliding had its origin in the discovery that gliders can stay airborne for long periods, cover long distances and reach great heights solely by exploiting the currents of the air. This manner of flight is called 'soaring' and gliders which soar are sometimes called 'sailplanes'.

To cut loose from the hills and soar across country, it is necessary to use a different kind of upcurrent from the localised one caused by wind blowing up a hill. Thermal currents or 'thermals' as they are called, consist of warmed air rising from sun heated ground and as the air goes up in a narrow stream, gliders (and birds) have to fly round in a tight circle to keep within its boundaries and get carried up with the rising current. When a thermal has risen a few thousand feet, a cumulus cloud may form at its top and in certain weather conditions these cumulus clouds may grow to enormous size, showers or even thunderstorms forming within them, with strong up-currents which can lift a glider tens of thousands of feet into the sky.

A glider flies in just the same way as a powered aeroplane, the flow of air over and under the wings providing lift. In a powered aeroplane speed is provided by the engine pulling it through the air. The glider or sailplane obtains its speed by

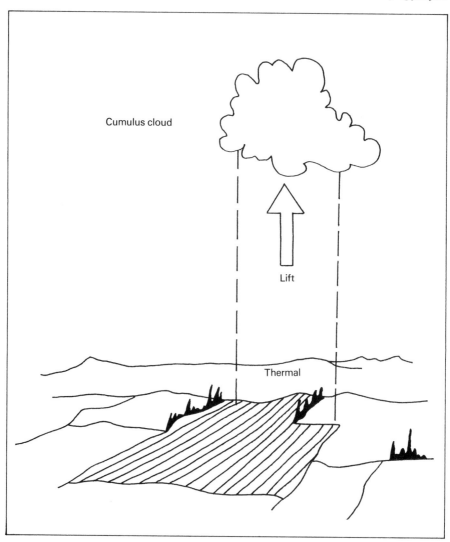

Cumulus cloud

Lift

Thermal

A thermal is a vertical column of warm rising air. When it reaches condensation level the water vapour it has been carrying may form a cumulus cloud.

gliding downhill, using gravity as engine power. If the glider pilot cannot find up-currents of air or 'thermals', he can only glide steadily downwards until he has reached the ground and has to land. If the pilot can find an up-current or 'thermal' of rising air which is ascending faster than he is descending, the glider will climb and thus gain height. This is known as soaring flight. A glider pilot soars across country by circling around in these 'thermals' and gaining height. Having used the 'thermal' in this manner, the pilot then flies in a straight line and often quite fast in the direction he wants to go. During this high speed run the pilot will be losing precious height, so he will be constantly on the look out for another 'thermal' to repeat the whole process before continuing on his way.

Most cross-country flights such as these are intended to finish at airfields or other gliding sites. Sometimes, however, the pilot runs out of lift and, when this happens he will have to select a suitable field or other landing area in which to land the glider. The pilot will then have to wait with his aircraft until collected by the retrieve crew when the glider will be brought home by road in its trailer. Before you can soar across country however, you must learn to glide.

Membership of a recognised gliding club carries with it associate membership of the British Gliding Association, whose working funds are derived from a levy of all member clubs. There are now a large number of these civilian gliding clubs in Britain and a list of addresses can be found at the back of this book. The lower age limit for solo flying is 16 years, though a 15-year-old may fly a glider if he or she is accompanied by an instructor.

Pilots' Licences and Certificates

No formal pilot's licence is required to fly a glider or sailplane. Instead a series of certificates and badges are awarded to denote a certain level of achievement and to acknowledge the completion of certain tasks. As far as a newcomer to the sport is concerned, his first aim will be to achieve his 'A' or 'solo' certificate. This will be awarded after the student has been allowed to fly solo, usually after a few hours of dual flying instruction. He will then be entitled to wear a badge with a single white bird in silhouette on a blue disc. The 'B' certificate requires the completion of three solo flights, with turns in both directions. This adds another white bird to the badge, making two in the silhouette. To attempt the

The glider and its components.

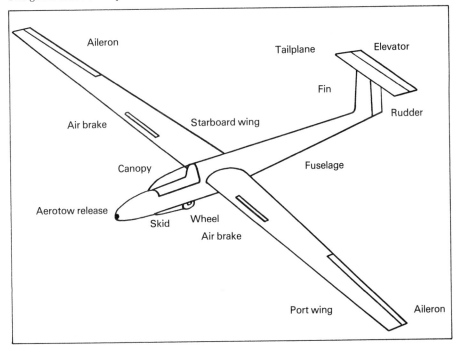

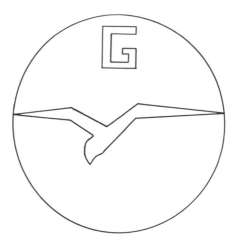

The 'A' badge for glider pilots.

'C' or soaring badge, the applicant must hold both 'A' and 'B' certificates. The test for this badge requires the pilot to carry out a soaring flight of at least five minutes followed by a normal landing.

Medical requirements

No formal medical examination is required by British Gliding Association rules. Instead, glider and sailplane pilots are asked to submit a formal statement of health, like that on a driving licence application form. The questions mainly concern freedom from faintness or giddyness, adequate vision (being able to read a car number plate at 23 m (25 yds) is the usual requirement), or any other medical condition that might affect a student glider pilot's ability to fly a glider safely. Disqualification from flying is not automatic if you are not able to sign the declaration, but the gliding club may require further medical information before you will be allowed to fly.

A Vega glider showing its retractable undercarriage.

Part A
TO BE SIGNED BEFORE STARTING
TO FLY AS A PUPIL OR SOLO
PILOT

I hereby declare that I have never
suffered from any of the following
which may create or lead to a
dangerous situation in flight.

Epilepsy, fits, fainting, giddiness or
blackouts, unusually high blood
pressure, diabetes, psychiatric disorder,
adrenal or other glandular disorders,
previous major head injury, multiple
sclerosis, a previous coronary, any
conditions requiring the regular use of
drugs.

I further declare that in the event of my
contracting or suspecting any of the
above conditions, I will cease to fly
until I have obtained medical opinion.

Signed _____ Date _____

Name in block letters _____

_____

If you cannot sign the above
declaration, you must before flying
obtain the signature of your regular
General Practitioner.

I am the regular GP of the applicant. I
understand the applicant wishes to fly
sporting gliders, but has been unable to
sign the declaration. In my opinion it is
safe for him/her to do so.

Signed _____

Date _____

Name and address _____

_____

Applicant's name_____

Part B
The following conditions may affect
your comfort when flying gliders. If
you suffer or have suffered from any
of the following you are advised to
seek medical opinion.

Chronic bronchitis, severe asthma,
pneumathorax, rheumatic fever, any
chronic disorder of the bone joints,
chronic ear or sinus disease.

It is also advisable that if you normally
wear glasses you should always carry a
readily accessible spare pair.

Formal statement of health called for by the British Gliding Association.

Clothing

In summer, although it can be very warm on the ground, the air temperature at
a couple of thousand feet can be much colder. So sunbathing gear is not really
all that suitable. Don't forget that airfields are exposed places, often with more

Above *A modern glider such as this Vega may cost £10,000.*

Left *The cockpit of a Slingsby Vega.*

Above right *The Sport Vega.*

wind than elsewhere, so take care not to get sunburned. Sunglasses are almost essential and in really hot weather, a hat when you are flying (without too floppy a brim, the instructor in the rear seat has to see around you) will protect your head from the glare and heat through the canopy. In winter, a warm anorak or coat, slacks, cap and gloves. Mittens are not advisable for flying, as they restrict the 'feel' of the glider's controls. For the same reason very heavy shoes or boots are not recommended, although it is essential to have warm, comfortable and waterproof footwear. Cold, wet feet on an airfield will ruin your enjoyment of the day's gliding.

Social activities

All gliding clubs have a variety of lectures, film shows, dances and disco parties throughout the year. There is always plenty of room for a variety of new skills be they technical, culinary, organisational or secretarial. Don't be shy about being new to a club, your offer of help will be more than welcome. Most gliding clubs have meals and refreshments available in the clubhouse at reasonable prices and some also have a licensed bar.

Learning to Glide

Anyone aged 16 years or over may fly a glider provided he or she is able to sign the declaration of physical fitness. There are various ways in which you can learn to glide. It will not take you very long if you are already a qualified power pilot with experience of flying light aeroplanes or helicopters. But in any case, whatever your previous experience, it is a good idea to visit a gliding club and have a trial flight before committing yourself to joining as a full flying member. Learning to fly gliders is best accomplished by starting on a holiday course of one or two weeks duration. This is the quickest way to reach solo standard, but it is only by flying regularly that you will become a really proficient glider pilot. If your flying lessons are separated by more than a week, learning to fly a glider can be a slow and time-consuming process. However, having joined the nearest gliding club, the new pilot will soon discover that the more willing he or she is to

Above *A Cirrus glider prepares for launch.* **Above right** *Ready for launch.*

help with getting gliders out of the hanger and over to the launch point, keeping the flight log sheet, running at the wingtips and helping with the launch and pushing gliders back to the launch point after landing, the more flying he or she will get. If you want to book an aircraft and have it waiting for you to step into, you should forget about gliding and take up powered flying instead. For your first few flights you do need good weather conditions to make quick progress. Any dry day without low cloud and with a light wind will be suitable for the beginner. If the weather is too bad to fly when you arrive at the club, do not return home, you can learn many interesting things just by talking to other students and instructors and the more knowledge you can assimilate about gliding the quicker you will learn and the more time and money you will save.

Your early flights will be made with the instructor explaining what the glider is doing, how the controls are moved and so on. You will notice as the control stick is moved forward the nose of the glider goes down, the airspeed increases and the glider descends. When the stick is eased back the nose of the glider comes up and the airspeed decreases. Ease the stick to the left and the left wing will drop and the right wing will rise up causing the glider to bank to the left. Conversely by easing the control stick to the right, the right wing will drop and the left wing will rise up causing the glider to bank to the right. These four movements are known as the primary effects of control. On these early flights you may experience some occasionally vivid sensations. The air is rarely still and while you are flying you will often be tipped slightly, this way and that by the bumps and currents in the air. While you are getting used to the glider and its controls these upsets can be rather disconcerting, but eventually you will correct for them with the controls, smoothly and automatically without thinking, rather like driving a motorcar. We all have an inborn fear of falling and contrary to your expectations, when flying gliders you will not experience the same sensation one gets when looking down from a high building or cliff edge.

The standard cockpit check list for gliders is memorised by the initials CBSIFTCB, and is as follows:

C = controls. Do the stick and rudder pedals move correctly, fully and freely, not obstructed by cushions, maps etc?

B = ballast. Is the weight correct? A glider will only fly safely if the weight is within limits stated on the flight limitations label. This must be checked and ballast added if the pilot does not weigh enough.

S = straps. Are the seat harness straps of both student and instructor fastened correctly?

I = instruments. Instruments must be undamaged and the altimeter set correctly.

F = flaps (if fitted). Is the flap setting correct? They should be set for take off.

T = trim. Does the trim lever move fully and freely? It should be set for take off.

C = canopy. Is the canopy closed and locked?

B = brakes. Are the airbrakes closed? In a stiff wind it may be prudent to leave the airbrakes open while on the ground, but they should be closed and locked before launch.

The take off

As soon as the student glider pilot is able to handle the aircraft in the air, he or she can start learning the take off drill. There are basically three ways in use of launching gliders—aerotowing, car and winch launching. Aerotowing is a method where a powered aircraft will tow the glider by means of a cable joining the two aircraft up to a height of 610 m (2,000 ft). Although the aerotow gives more height in which to practice turns, stalls, spins, etc, the tow itself requires more skill on behalf of the pilot than a car or winch launch. The important thing is to keep the wings level, keep in position behind the towing aircraft and react to any slight change and correct for it immediately. You should also make sure you know the emergency signals used when aerotowing. If at the end of the launch you cannot release the tow cable, pull over to the left hand side behind the tug plane and tell its pilot by rocking the wings of the glider. If the tug plane rocks its wings, you must release the towing cable at once.

Car and winch launching provide very simple and economical ways of launching gliders up to a height of around 300 m (1,000 ft). As the student pilot, you will find these launches ideal for training purposes, as at this stage you will require practice in circuit flying and take off and landing procedure, rather than soaring flight. With any of these methods of launching, there is the remote

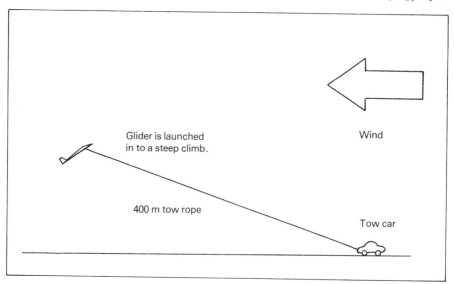

Glider is launched
in to a steep climb.

Wind

400 m tow rope

Tow car

Above *Tow car glider launching.* **Above right** *Aerotow glider launching.* **Below** *A glider at the start of a winch launch. The small parachute is to lower the cable after release.*

possibility of mechanical failure. Should the steel cable break whilst launching, the immediate action is to lower the nose of the glider, drop the remains of the cable and to decide quickly if there is room to land ahead or whether a turn will have to be made to enable the glider to put down in the nearest convenient open space. Some points to bear in mind when practising launches and landings are as follows:

Aerotow launches

  1 Use gentle movements on the controls.

  2 Keep your wings level with those of the tug plane.

  3 Check the tow rope has released before turning off.

  4 In the event of a poor launch, always check your airbrakes to make sure they are closed and locked.

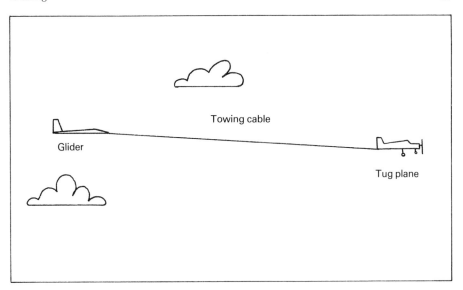

Towing cable

Glider

Tug plane

Car and winch launches

1 Lower the nose of the glider before pulling the cable release.

2 Think before you take off, what will you do if the cable breaks.

The landing

A good landing is made from a high, straight approach at the correct speed. The idea is gradually to reduce the path of the aircraft from a steep glide so that when it arrives over the landing point, it will be in the correct altitude and at stalling speed. If the flare is made too high, the glider will sink heavily on to the ground. If it is made too low, it will strike its landing wheel and bounce, resulting in a longer landing run. As the glider approaches the ground, the pilot should look well ahead, judging his height by what he can see from the corner of his eyes and adjusting with the control stick as necessary. To achieve a good landing the glider should touch down on its mainwheel and tail skid at the same time. It must then be kept running straight, with the wings level until the speed decreases and the glider comes to a halt, when one wing will gently drop to the ground. The glider pilot's experience up to this point will have been confined to flying a straightforward circuit, describing the shape of an oblong, with a launch crosswind turn, downwind leg, base leg and final turn and landing (see figure overleaf).

The first solo

Most student glider pilots think they are ready to fly solo before being sent off to do so by their instructor. But when he actually steps out of the cockpit and casually tells you to take it round the circuit by yourself, you will be caught by surprise. As the launching cable is hooked on and you go through your cockpit check, you hear your voice seemingly distant saying ready for launch. The cable becomes taut and the glider starts to move forward, the man at the wingtip is suddenly left running far behind. The speed settles at around 50-55 knots and the nose of the aircraft comes up and begins to climb. The control stick is pulled further and further back as the glide angle steepens and the altimeter unwinds

towards the 300 m (1,000 ft) marker. As you reach the desired height the nose of
the glider is lowered and with a click the cable is released. Now you realise you
do not have your instructor with you, it is you that is flying this aircraft on your
own. However, the circuit is no place for day-dreaming and you must now busy
yourself with the pre-landing checks. You turn the glider on to base leg and then
on to final approach. The dive brakes come open with a bang and a roar,
holding the speed to around 55 knots in the dive. You suddenly recall that in a
glider you are committed on the first approach, you can't go round again and if
you undershoot the landing, too bad. The landing field is now floating up to
meet you, the control stick is eased back gently, rounding out the glider a foot
or so above the ground. The grass flashes past the canopy in a speeding blur and
with a small bump you are down. For a few moments there is a horrendous

Below *Planning the glider's landing approach.* **Right** *A glider circuit.*

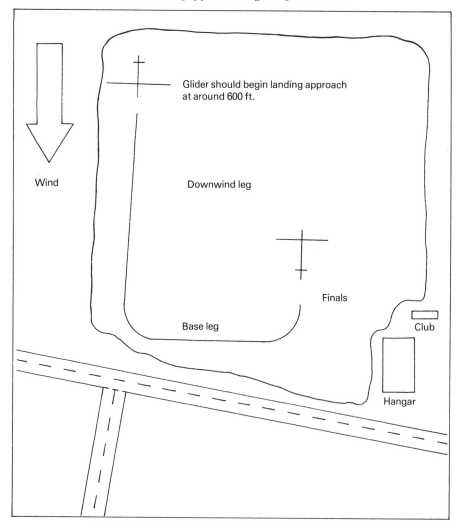

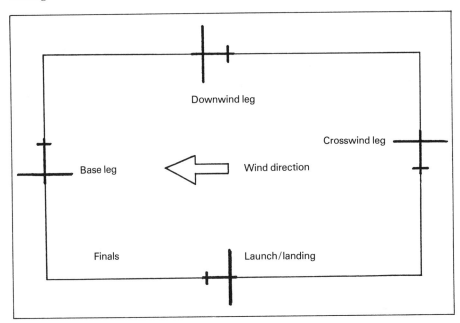

bumping and crashing on the uneven surface as the glider runs to a stop. With a gentle sigh a wingtip dips to the ground and all is quiet once more.

An enormous grin of self congratulation spreads over your face as fellow club members cluster around the aircraft to ask you what it was like. You tell them it was great, for you have 'soloed' and it is an experience that can never be repeated. You will now consolidate your flight with a couple more solo circuits, just to prove the first was not a fluke. But like thousands of other pilots before you, you have now passed the magic barrier of the first solo flight.

Examination for the bronze 'C'

The next stage in the glider pilot's training will come when he is judged ready to tackle the examination for the bronze 'C'. When this has been completed it gives the privilege of leaving the circuit and embarking on cross-country flights. This qualification is, in fact, a full gliding licence. The examination syllabus laid down by the British Gliding Association for the bronze 'C' is split into five sections as follows:

Principles of flight
Demonstrate an elementary under-standing of:
(a) Aerofoils.
(b) Lift and drag.
(c) Forces acting during flight.
(d) Turning.
(e) Stalling.
(f) Spinning.
(g) Loading (placard speeds).
(h) Effects of controls (axes).
(i) Further effects of controls.
(j) Stability.

Meteorology
Demonstrate an elementary under-standing of:
(a) Fronts (recognition of approach, associated pressure changes, order of stability).
(b) Convection.
(c) Cloud formation (lapse rates, condensation levels).
(d) Weather maps (basic understanding of signs and symbols).
(e) Gliding aspects (hill lift, wave lift and thermal soaring).
(f) Forecasts.

Navigation
(a) Map reading.
(b) Appreciation of cross-country flying, the effect of wind on track and groundspeed.
(c) Field landings.
(d) Understanding of the compass (deviation and variation, turning and acceleration errors).
(e) Vector triangles.
(f) Geographical appreciation (true and magnetic north, lines of longtitude and latitude, the distribution of pressure in the northern and southern hemispheres).

Instruments
Demonstrate an elementary understanding of instruments, their construction and uses:
(a) ASI (airspeed indicator).
(b) Altimeter.
(c) Variometer.
(d) Errors.

Airmanship and general knowledge
(a) Full knowledge of air law.
(b) Ground handling and signals.

The Air Test
The candidate must have made two soaring flights, each of more than 30 minutes' duration, when launched by winch or tow car, or of 60 minutes' duration after launch from an aerotow not exceeding a height of 600 m (2,000 ft). This must be followed by a normal landing into a designated landing area. He must have completed a minimum of two dual flights, satisfactorily demonstrating an understanding of stalling and spinning and the correct recovery procedures, accurate general flying and two field landings or landings into a marked-off enclosure on the gliding field without reference to his altimeter.

On achieving the bronze 'C', the newly qualified pilot can add a small bronze filigree to his badge. There are further badges and distinctions to be gained, one of these being the silver 'C', which roughly a quarter of this country's glider pilots are entitled to wear.

Holiday courses
A good way to learn gliding is to take a holiday course at one of the many clubs and schools that offer this tuition. These courses usually run from April through to September and a list of participating clubs can be obtained from the British Gliding Association, Kimberley House, Vaughn Way, Leicester LE1 4SG (tel Leicester (0533) 51051).

Some of these clubs have residential accommodation at the flying field, others will arrange for you to stay at a nearby inn or hotel. A tent or caravan may also be allowed on to the gliding site, the individual clubs will be happy to provide further details. With facilities varying from club to club there can be no set prices. Costs may range from £80 for a five-day all-inclusive course in Scotland to £230 for the same thing in Hampshire. For a 'Flying Only' course that is all flying tuition and club fees, but not including meals or accommodation, weekly prices may start at around £50 according to club, district and season. Typical flying fees at a gliding club may work out something like this (1983).

Winch launch		£1.20
Aero tows (2 seater)	£3.00 to 1,000 ft	17 p per 100 ft
(1 seater)	£2.80 to 1,000 ft	14 p per 100 ft
Flying time		8p per minute
Motor Falke		18p per minute

For the newcomer to the sport who wishes to fly solo during his course, two

Coming in on final approach.

consecutive weeks would be recommended. An intensive gliding course is a faster way to reach solo standard in a short space of time, rather than just training at weekends, but you will need to fly regularly to remain a competent pilot. As with weekend flying the holiday student will be expected to pull his or her weight with the various ground tasks such as cable retrieving and glider rigging.

Equipment
The glider
Most modern gliders are now made of glass fibre. The vast majority of clubs and schools, however, are equipped with older wood and fabric machines. These are not only less expensive than the fibre glass types, but are easier for the inexperienced student to learn on, thanks to their higher drag designs and more docile handling qualities. The wooden glider may be constructed all of wood or may be a mix of plywood and welded steel tube. These gliders do not give as high a performance as the more modern machines which have lower drag designs. They are, however, quite adequate for general club flying, where speed and cross-country flying are not the prime requirements. These aircraft usually have a fixed undercarriage and airbrakes only, not being fitted with items such as flaps or braking parachutes. A number of clubs are now turning to motor gliders such as the motor Falke. Learning takes less time as there is no waiting for launching cables or suitable weather to develop.

For the enthusiast interested in owning his or her own glider, the usual form is to join a syndicate. Thus for a few hundred pounds, a pilot can buy, say, a one sixth share in an older type machine and take turns in flying it. Becoming a syndicate member also means looking after the aircraft and its trailer and you will be expected to put in a good few hours work on ground maintenance. While gliders are immensely strong in the air, they can be easily damaged on the ground. Gliders should never be pushed on or held by the trailing edge of the wing, the tailplane or any of the control surfaces.

Parachutes

People often wonder why glider pilots wear parachutes when light aircraft pilots do not. Although modern gliders are very safe, the seat is designed as a form of 'bucket' into which the parachute fits and becomes the cushion on which to sit, rather like a modern jet fighter aircraft. Gliders are strongly constructed, but they may enter storm clouds when soaring cross country, so the wearing of a parachute is only a safety precaution.

Code of Practice

The gliding fraternity owes a great deal to farmers for the help their pilots have received when the thermals have run out and a glider has had to make a field landing on private property. All due care must be taken to cause as little damage as possible. Gates should be kept shut. Standing crops and livestock should be avoided. Interested members of the public should also be restrained from trampling some farmer's potato crop, in order to get a look at the glider which has just dropped out of the sky. The farmer or landowner should be notified of your arrival in his field and vehicles should be kept out until permission to proceed has been obtained. Follow the country code at all times.

Chapter 4

Hang gliding

Man has always dreamed of the day when he might put on wings and fly like the birds. Modern aviation, however, does not fulfill the original vision of flight, the solitary man spreading his wings to soar through the sky. The basic concept of the hang glider dates back hundreds of years. One of the first hang glider pilots was a Benedictine monk who launched himself from the tower of Malmesbury Abbey only to crash in the next field. With the coming of the Renaissance era and its scientific genius Leonardo Da Vinci, aerodynamics and scientific study were applied to the problem of flight. This resulted in Da Vinci's construction of model 'ornithopters' around the year 1490. The resemblance between these models and today's Rogallo hang gliders is remarkable. The Rogallo glider was developed by Francis Rogallo as part of a design for a re-entry vehicle for the National Aeronautics and Space Administration (NASA). When hang gliding first became popular on the west coast of America in the 1960s, it was on this delta wing design that the early pioneers based their machines. Back in those days construction techniques were pretty simple, a v-shaped frame was made of bamboo poles and covered with polythene sheeting. As in the early days of aviation, it is no wonder that pilots were killed attempting to fly these primitive aircraft. As the sport has now developed into a worldwide cult interest, many manufacturers now turn out commercially constructed machines of an extremely safe and strong design. For the person who cannot afford the more expensive forms of aviation such as light aircraft or helicopters, flying a hang glider is one of the least expensive ways of getting into the air.

First steps

For the pilot hang gliding is immensely challenging and very personal. He is not bothered with aerodrome regulations or air traffic controllers, he is on his own and his safety is solely his concern. But how do you begin?

The first step is to visit the local library and read everything on hang gliding you can find. Contact the British Hang Gliding Association, telling them you are interested in taking up the sport and wish to learn more. They will send you an information pack consisting of a list of hang gliding clubs nationwide, so you can find the nearest one to you, a leaflet giving general information on training, clothing, fitness, etc. and an application form for membership of the BHGA. If you have not flown any sort of aircraft before, you will have to put aside for a while the thought of 'stepping lightly off a grassy hilltop and gliding

Above *A good pilot makes it look easy.* **Opposite page** *This is what hang gliding is about.*

out into the valley' as it says in so many glossy brochures and newspaper articles. Learning to fly involves hard work and study and it is no different with hang gliding.

First you will need to find a good club or school from which to take instruction. This should be as near to your home as possible to save unnecessary travelling. Most clubs and schools run two- and four-day courses. Both are very useful ways of learning to hang glide, but if you can spare the time, the four-day course will train a person up to elementary standard or pilot 1 as it is known. This is the basic award of the BHGA, presented to a beginner in hang gliding. It tells a club or manufacturer what standard the person has obtained, enabling them to advise accordingly if the weather is suitable for him to fly on a particular day or if the glider he or she wants to buy is suitable for the experience level attained. It is preferable to take one of these full-time courses of instruction where possible and to follow up by flying every weekend for a few months thereafter to stay proficient. By concentrated learning in this manner, you will achieve experience of hang gliding in different wind and weather conditions. It is possible to learn to fly just by coming along at weekends, and indeed many people learn to glide in this manner. This method, however, can be a slow and frustrating way of learning.

When you first attend the hang gliding school you will probably spend the first day on the ground, learning the various procedures of flight in a suspended mock up of the hang glider harness. In this way the various techniques of controlling the glider's attitude by weight shift can be learned without risk to yourself or others. You will be shown how to take off, turn and flare for landing. Many schools also make use of videos and cine films and these are a useful training aid as they show instructors and other experienced pilots taking

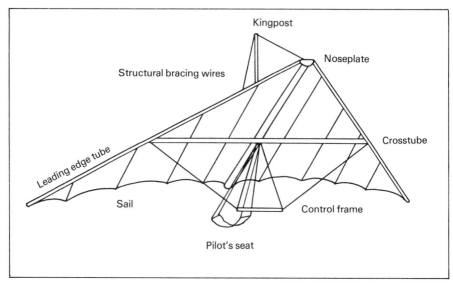

Above *The hang glider and its components.* **Below** *A hill provides lift only when the wind is blowing almost directly on to it.* **Above right** *Launching from the hillside.*

off, flying and landing and you can gain an understanding of what it is you will be trying to do. Your instructor will also give you a basic lesson on aerodynamics and the theory of flight. He or she will demonstrate with the use of a model, how the hang glider flies, how the airflow past the wing provides lift and what happens if you should fly too slowly and the glider stalls.

When you first start learning you will begin with a series of small bird-like hops, gradually working up the hill as your ability increases. To help the new pilot get flying on his own as soon as possible, a number of hang gliding schools are now using a method called tethered flying. This is a very simple system in which the hang glider has long lines attached to its nose and wingtips and are held by the instructor and pupils. The advantage of this system is that training can be carried out when strong winds would put a stop to free flying. If you learn to fly without being tethered, this means you will start with less strong winds. Constant wind strengths are quite satisfactory, but gusting presents a real danger, particularly at the point of take off or landing. Many schools and clubs also use a small VHF radio to talk to the student pilot in flight. This is done via a small radio receiver fitted inside the helmet. As you progress and you move further up the hill, you will be taught how to turn the hang glider to the left or to the right. This is so that you can turn the glider into wind before landing. While you are flying you will encounter drift. Remember the wind will not always be blowing straight along your landing area. You will therefore need to allow for wind drift in order to land at your intended point. Failure to do so may see you on the ground sooner and considerably harder than you intended.

The glider
As we have mentioned before, a hang glider is a basic aircraft of a simple design. Control varies from weight shift on the Rogallo gliders to simple aerodynamic controls as fitted to powered aircraft. The hang glider does not take very long to rig for flying. The primary frame is made of aluminium tube and bolted together and braced with stainless steel wires. It is extremely

Above *Hang glider in soaring flight.* **Below right** *Two-'seater' trainer in soaring flight.*

important that the hang glider is rigged according to the manufacturer's instructions and no experimental adjustments or additions are made. Do not consider home building a hang glider unless you know a great deal about flexible wing aerodynamics and airworthiness requirements. A good second-hand glider can be bought for less than the cost of materials needed to build one. Therefore you should always purchase your machine from a reputable dealer.

Pilot's licence

The British Hang Gliding Association does not require a formal pilot's licence; instead a series of certificates and badges are awarded as the pilot climbs up the ratings ladder. These range from the elementary or P1 certificate to the FAI Delta Gold which requires a distance flight of 300 kilometres (186 miles).

Medical requirements

There is no formal medical examination to undergo. All the prospective pilot is required to do is declare himself free of any major disorders such as chest or heart troubles, high blood pressure, diabetes, blackouts, fits or dizzy spells when he or she books a course of instruction. For any energetic sport you must be fit and active and hang gliding is no exception. If you have any doubts about your general fitness, get the advice of your local GP before you fly.

What to wear

Even in summer it can be cold on the hills used for hang gliding. Take enough warm and windproof clothes with you, plus comfortable waterproof footwear that give good grip and some ankle support (not the lacehook variety) and gloves which will not slip on the control bar. While you are training the school or club will provide you with a crash helmet, but it is up to you to check that it fits properly and it is wise thereafter to purchase your own.

Flying with a club

If you enjoyed your training course you will want to go on flying and the best way to do this is to join a club. Tell the club coach how much flying you have done and if you have already bought a hang glider, what sort it is. He and other experienced members of the club will tell you when to fly and when to stay on the ground. Expect to progress slowly at first. You will have a new hang glider to get used to and a new flying site to explore. Your experience up to this point will have been limited *so don't rush it.* Don't fly just anywhere, as you could endanger not only yourself, but also the right to fly for many others as well as yourself.

Costs

The cost of learning to hang glide varies enormously from school to school, but the average cost for a four-day full-time course is somewhere between £60 and £100. A shorter two-day introductory course is also available and the price of this is usually between £30 and £50. Alternatively instruction may be taken on a daily basis, the charge usually being around £16 (1983 prices). A discount may

Above *Taking off. The hands should be placed comfortably and firmly to exert control.*
Above right *The hang glider feels buoyant when it takes off into lift.*

be given if a group booking is taken. Individual clubs and schools will be happy to supply further details.

Rules

There are not many rules in hang gliding. You will have to learn the law on collision avoidance and the various airspace regulations. There are a few BHGA rules, but it is mostly a matter of applying common sense. The minimum age for hang gliding is 16 years of age. It is very true to say that while hang gliding is not forgiving of fools, it is as safe or as dangerous as you, the individual, wish to make it. With the proper tuition and equipment, it is safe. With unsuitable equipment and the wrong approach, it can be dangerous.

Most hang glider manufacturers will not sell you a new or used hang glider unless you hold an elementary or P1 certificate. Obsolete or dangerous hang gliders are occasionally offered for sale, so for your own sake get advice before you buy. Have the glider inspected by the club's or manufacturer's technical officer to make sure it is fully airworthy and that no unorthodox modifications have been carried out. The association publishes its own magazine *Wings* and carries a selection of new and used hang gliders for sale in its small advertisements column. It is available from the address at the back of this book. As with conventional gliders a code of good practice has been set up.

A flight should never be attempted alone, either by expert or beginner for even a minor injury sustained in a remote area could create a serious situation if there were no help at hand. Finding a suitable and accessible site from which to fly is not always easy. Permission to glide must be obtained in advance or there may be opposition from local people. Do not fly from a site where there are livestock in the landing area. Use only recognised gates and close them after you; do not climb through hedges. Avoid standing crops, if you do land in them

minimise your movements and cause the least amount of damage possible. Keep members of the public out. If your hang gliding is likely to cause traffic congestion inform the local police. Designate landing areas and take off points and keep them free of spectators.

Wear a crash helmet on every flight. The following standards are acceptable for hang gliding: BS 5361, BS 2495. Helmets should be a close fit and secured by a strap that passes under the jaw.

Soaring flight
Soaring flights are achieved by flying the hang glider in thermals or hill lift. Thermals are currents of warm air rising from the heated ground. They rise

Soaring at 2,000 ft. Note instruments on control frame.

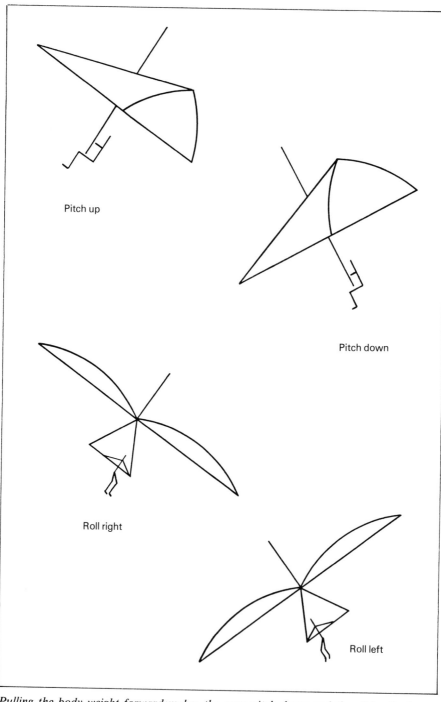

Pitch up

Pitch down

Roll right

Roll left

Pulling the body weight forward makes the nose pitch down and the glider fly faster. Pushing the body weight back pitches the nose up and reduces speed. To roll left, move body weight to the left. To move right, move body weight to the right.

higher and higher until they cool to the temperature of the surrounding air. A good indication of thermal activity is the formation of cumulus cloud. Unless the surrounding air is very dry and devoid of moisture, one of these clouds will more than likely form at the top of each thermal. In thermal soaring, the hang glider pilot must stick to the 'inner core' of maximum lift, by circling around in it. A challenge to this type of flying is 'thermal turbulence' caused by large warm air masses moving upwards and being replaced by cooler descending air. In these conditions a hang glider and pilot's performance are put to the test. A hang glider because of its extremely light construction is far more sensitive to turbulence, however light, than any other form of aircraft.

One of the other types of soaring is hill or ridge lift. As the wind blows through a valley it will encounter a hill and rise up over it. The best type of hill for this sort of flying is one that has a rounded crest and a flatish top on which to land. The theory is to traverse back and forth along the hill and flights of several hours' duration have been achieved by this method. If the hill falls away to the rear, beware of flying here for there will most likely be vicious downdraughts that may throw you and your glider to the ground very hard indeed. The top of cliffs especially when jagged have these eddies and wind rotors which are capable of smashing hang gliders to pieces and are best left, therefore, to the experts.

When you do begin to make soaring flights, you will soon discover one thing which up to now you will have not been airborne long enough to experience. The air is cold. Flying in cold winds is not only uncomfortable it can also be dangerous. For the same reason a swimmer immersed in cold water will get fatigued, so will the hang glider pilot in cold air. The cold affects the brain, slowing down reaction time and creeping into the muscles. Remember, it is better on a cold day to make several shorter flights, than one long one.

The British Hang Gliding Association pilot rating system
Pilot 1 rating

As we have said, to protect newcomers to the sport, schools and manufacturers have agreed not to sell hang gliders to those below pilot 1 standard. To obtain the pilot 1 certificate the hang glider pilot must complete the following tasks:

1 The correct rigging procedure and pre flight inspection of his hang glider and harness without prompting.

2 15 solo flights with a ground clearance of at least 12 m (40 ft).

3 During each of the three final qualifying flights: (a) well executed unassisted take offs; (b) the flying of a planned flight path with well executed 90 degree turns to the left and the right; (c) stand up landings in a pre-designated landing area.

The final three qualifying flights must have a ground clearance of at least 30 m (100 ft) from a take off point not less than 60 m (200 ft) above the landing area.

On his final qualifying flight the pilot must demonstrate proper recovery from a mild stall from straight and level flight at a safe height before completing 3(b) and 3(c).

4 An ability to fly safely in steady winds of up to 18 knots and in gusty conditions of up to 10 knots where the wind speed variation does not exceed 6 knots.

5 He must pass the BHGA test on the following subjects: the code of good practice; the flying rules; the flying recommendations; the student syllabus.

Opposite page *To obtain the best performance, the pilot flies in the prone position to reduce the drag from his body.*

The pilot will have copies of all these and be able to discuss or demonstrate (where practicable) any points relating to the above subjects.

In completing the above tasks the pilot must demonstrate to the BHGA instructor that he is of a required standard of airmanship to continue his flying training both safely and competently.

Pilot 2 rating

Before applying for a pilot 2 rating the pilot must have held a pilot 1 rating for at least four months. The pilot must safely demonstrate:

1 Thirty flights, of at least 10 minutes' duration, each flight must be separately logged.

2 Five flights from each of five different sites, of which at least three are inland.

3 Ten five minute flights, five from each of two different sites.

4 Two stand up top landings on each of three different sites, two of which must be inland.

5 Three stand up landings, within a 12 m (40 ft) diameter area, after flights of at least one minute's duration. These landings may be top landings.

6 Three nil wind take offs, ending in stand up landings.

7 The flying of the FAI delta bronze tasks.

8 Precise 180 degree turns, both gently and steeply banked, to the left and right.

Practice in landing accurately is always valuable.

Discuss and safely demonstrate:

9 Good control in turns; stall recovery from straight and level flight into wind; recognition of the onset of a stall and its prevention in a positive manner; how to cope with wind gradient and the importance of airspeed on a landing approach; the crosswind tracking top landing method.

Discuss and show a thorough understanding of: the BHGA code of good practice, flying rules and recommendations; glide angle control (not parachuting); spin, yaw and side slip recovery; the three top landing approach methods (crosswind tracking, downwind, glide angle control with strong winds) and their associated advantages and dangers in certain conditions; the stall when flying downwind, its recognition, prevention and recovery and its implications in turns near the ground; the effects of wind gradient and gusts in both upwind and downwind flight; the effects of upwind terrain features and the flow of air over obstructions; different flying characteristics and pilot requirements of the hang gliders that are operated within the club; how to cope with difficult weather conditions on club flying sites.

Pass the BHGA examination on: air law, navigation and meteorology applicable to the flying of hang gliders particularly on cross country flights within a pilot's 'local' area.

Pilot 3 rating

Before applying for a pilot 3 rating the pilot must have held a pilot 2 rating for at least four months.

High altitude: The pilot must make one flight during which the terrain clearance exceeds 300 m (1,000 ft) for at least ten minutes. Well coordinated turns must be accomplished in both directions. He must have flown at altitudes exceeding 200 m (650 ft) for a minimum of ten minutes' duration out of ridge lift and displaying good thermalling techniques.

Duration: The pilot must make five one hour soaring flights, two being prone or supine from a minimum of three different sites. He must have logged 25 hours' flying time on hang gliders. At least half these hours must be completed on a hang glider with an aspect ratio of 4.5 or less.

Cross country: The pilot must make three cross country distance flights of at least 10, 20 and 30 kilometres (6, 12 and 18 miles) between take off and landing. He must be able to explain and discuss in detail how to cope with the following problems: the determination of upper and lower wind directions from natural sources whilst in flight; the setting up of conservative planned approaches to unfamiliar landing areas and the allowance of a sufficient margin of error for unexpected changes in the circumstances; wind, turbulence, sheer and lift conditions met in various regions, such as valleys, mountains, woodland and built-up areas.

Precision flying: The pilot must demonstrate three top landing methods, ie, cross wind tracking approach, glide angle approach control, an approach involving a downwind leg at a safe height. He must discuss all the advantages and disadvantages involved with each of the above methods and give conditions for the use of each.

Theoretical requirements: The pilot must pass a BHGA written examination on: air law; navigation; meteorology; principles of flight.

Taking the above written examinations will finalise the pilot 3 rating. This will indicate that the hang glider pilot has reached advanced level and has shown maturity and judgement to act prudently so as not to be a hazard to himself or other users or airspace on any sites he or she may visit.

FAI Delta Silver

A distance flight of not less than 50 kilometres (30 miles), this distance to be measured in a straight line. A height of not less than 1,000 m (3,280 ft) must be gained above the launch height. A flight of at least five hours' duration. The above may be performed separately or on the same flight.

FAI Delta Gold

A distance flight of 300 kilometres (186 miles). An out and return, or a triangle flight of 200 kilometres (122 miles).

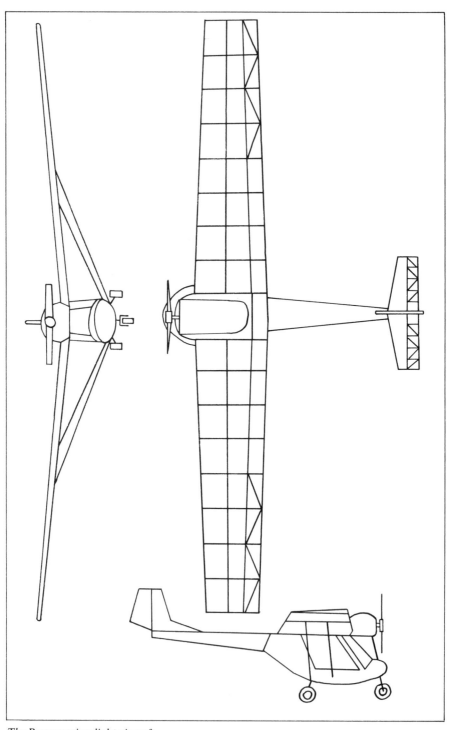

The Ranger microlight aircraft.

Chapter 5

The microlight

If you want to go flying for fun in a lightweight powered aircraft and yet don't have a fortune to spend, then microlight aircraft are for you. Purchase and running costs are well within the range of the average pocket and you could learn to fly at a microlight school near you. Depending on your natural ability, you could be flying competently in just a few dry, light wind days. It is a few years now since microlight aircraft first began to appear on the British aviation scene. The accepted definition of a microlight aircraft is an aeroplane having an empty weight not exceeding 150 kg (303 lb) and a wing area in no case less than 10 square metres (12 sq yds). Some of the machines on the market, advertised as microlights, do not in fact meet this requirement and must therefore be registered with the Civil Aviation Authority as 'aircraft' and flown by qualified pilots holding private pilot's licences or above. If you are in any doubt, consult the British Microlight Aircraft Association, E7 Stafford Park 4, Telford, Shropshire.

Training for the PPL (D)
The association has agreed a form of pilot licensing with the regulating authorities and it is known as the PPL Group D. To obtain the Private Pilot's Licence Group D, the student pilot must fly 25 hours, of which 10 hours must be as pilot in command of microlights. This training is usually tackled in two stages.

1 Training up to Part 'A' certificate, ie, 10 hours flying and the completion of certain tasks.

2 Training up to Part 'B' certificate (this is the full licence), ie, a further 15 hours flying including specified cross country flights.

The examination syllabuses for the ground tests are Air Law, Navigation and Meteorology and Aircraft Technical subjects. These have been specially drawn up for microlight pilots.

Resistance to these examinations appears to be losing ground within the microlight community. The general philosophy encouraged is that the more you know about aviation the better. Some schools and individuals connected with microlight flying say that the essence of the sport is freedom from rules and regulations, and they do not want the Civil Aviation Authority involved at all. Microlight aircraft, however, operate in the same airspace as civil and military powered aircraft and it is no good commercial and fighter pilots knowing the rules, if others do not.

Above *Flying high at 7,500 ft. Due to its excellent rate of climb, the Super Tiger Cub 440 will take you to 10,000 ft in ten minutes and cruise at 55 to 60 mph.* **Above right** *The two-seater Sky Ranger microlight.* **Below right** *A 'trike' being prepared for flight.*

Pilots who learn to fly at the outset on microlight aircraft are allowed quite large concessions if they later wish to fly conventional light aircraft and upgrade their licence from group 'D' to group 'A'. Instead of taking the full 43 hour PPL training course, they have to fly 18 hours, to include eight hours solo flying and nine hours dual flying. The converting pilot must also complete four hours dual instrument and three hours navigation flight. The full PPL qualifying cross country must also be completed. Flying instructors who are rated for conventional light aircraft, may also instruct on microlight aircraft. Qualified light aeroplane pilots can fly microlights, but would be well advised to take a conversion course first; some of the machines available may look conventional but they are different. Assistant and full flying instructor ratings have been established for microlights, paralleling the present set up for light aircraft, and will be supervised by the BMAA.

The aircraft

There are many types of microlight aircraft available in Britain, some British made, others imported from the USA or Australia. There are hang glider derivatives which give you the option to fly powered or use the glider alone for soaring. There are sophisticated three axis control machines similar to light aircraft, plus a whole range in between. Most people choose ready to fly aircraft, but some like the 'Ranger' or 'Tiger Cub' are available as kit construction models. In this way one can buy say a wing pack, assemble it and when you can afford it buy the next pack and so on. In this manner one can build a microlight in one's own time and spread the cost accordingly. Most microlight aircraft fold for car top transportation and generally require under ten minutes to prepare for flight.

When ready for flying, most microlights require comparatively short take off and landing strips. The first type of microlight aircraft is generally known as a

Above *The single-seater Lone Ranger microlight.* **Below right** *The Super Tiger Cub 440 all set for transportation with the MBA trailer. Light vans or cars from 1,000 cc engine capacity will comfortably tow the aircraft at 50 mph, even in strong motorway crosswinds. On arrival at the flying field the aircraft is rigged in five minutes before removing it from the trailer.*

'trike'. The trike is basically a powered hang glider and many are sold independently of the wing to which they have to be attached. A popular source of power for these machines is the 250 cc Fuji Robin single cylinder engine, mounted inverted to keep the centre of gravity low and increase control response. The drive is via three v-belts geared down by roughly 3 to 1 to a pusher propeller. A fuel tank of about two gallons capacity is mounted above the engine. Flying a trike is quite easy. The take off roll is very short—once the speed is up to around 18 mph the control bar is pushed forward to its limit and the aircraft is rotated off the ground. Once airborne, the control bar must be immediately pulled back into its midway position, the aircraft will then gain speed and climb away at about 30 mph.

Once in the air flying is simple and relaxed, with less concentration required than for other types of microlight machines. The approach and landing should be flown with plenty of speed, a burst of power just before landing will get the nose up and ensure a smooth touch down. The main advantage of this type of aircraft is its portability; most are transportable on the roof rack of the family car, thus avoiding the need for expensive hangerage.

The other main type of microlight is the three axis machine. These look pretty conventional in appearance with a wing either side, a tailplane with elevators and a fin and rudder. The power unit for these machines is a unit somewhere within the 20-45 hp range and drives either a pusher or puller propeller. Flying a three axis machine is very much like flying a conventional light aircraft, the only difference being roll control. On some three axis machines, this is provided by spoilers instead of by ailerons and are mounted one on the top of each wing. The take offs and landings are straightforward enough and spot landings can be carried out as required with power.

Medical requirements

There is a formal medical examination to undergo and this can be completed by the pilot's own doctor. It is similar to the light aircraft medical and like that certificate will last for two years if the pilot is under 40 and for one year if over that age.

The British Microlight Aircraft Association
The BMAA represents, in the widest sense those people interested in the operation of microlight aircraft in the United Kingdom. To be a strong organisation, the BMAA needs the support of all those involved with microlights, pilots, constructors, commercial bodies and all those still making up their minds about whether this is the type of sport they are looking for. The BMAAs magazine *Flight Line* is published bi-monthly and is circulated to members to provide a forum for views and information. There are now regular fly-ins taking place around the country which are enjoyable and educational for everyone involved. There is a single class of membership, currently (1983) costing around £15 per annum.

Learning to fly
Flying a microlight aircraft is exhilarating, fun, and above all else, cheap. Providing you receive proper training from the start it is also very safe. Freedom to fly demands responsibility, so a pilot must have a licence or be under training with the aim of obtaining one. There are a number of schools and clubs around the country offering training courses lasting from one hour to one week. You may wonder how you might take to microlight flying. There is no better way to find out than by taking ten minutes or so climbing up to 300 m (1,000 ft), and then leisurely gliding back down to earth, to put you fully in the picture. For the person who wants something a little more substantial than just a trial flight, there is a one-day introduction to microlights and this gives the prospective pilot a chance to see what will be required of him or her should they take up the sport. It will cover all aspects of microlight flying, usually through the use of videos or cine films and a practical flying demonstration. For anyone wishing to fly, the highlight of this course is a familiarisation flight in a two-seat microlight.

The five-day microlight course is aimed at giving full instruction for solo flight over five consecutive days. This will include the simple process of rigging and de-rigging an aircraft together with lectures in subjects such as Air Law,

Above *This photograph illustrates the exceptionally clean lines of the Super Tiger Cub 440 which enable the aircraft to maintain good ground speeds when flying into headwinds. The low drag also helps make possible its operating speed range of 30 to 80 mph.* **Below** *A Tiger Cub microlight flies over the early morning countryside.*

A simple 'trike' aircraft takes to the air.

Principles of Flight, Meteorology, Navigation and Map Reading. On the practical flying side, you will take to the air by the safe and proven auto-tow method. By this you will be airborne in a microlight without an engine. By means of a radio link from the towing vehicle to the aircraft, your instructor will coach you into a series of low level hops a few inches above the ground. As you develop skill and coordination in your flying, the length and height of each sortie is increased until you are flying the whole length of the runway at a height of around 60 feet. Familiarisation with the aerodrome circuit is then attained in a two-seat powered microlight, where you can begin to notice the various land-marks and points of interest in the surrounding countryside and gain perception in terms of height, approach speeds and angles.

Finally comes that magic first solo flight in a powered microlight, followed by practice in becoming a competent pilot in the finer points of flying. Weather conditions for solo training include a maximum wind speed of 10 mph, visibility of at least 5 kilometres (3 miles) and a minimum cloud base of 300 m (1,000 ft). Solo training flights must be flown within five miles of the take off point.

Costs

All aspects of microlight flying are far cheaper than conventional light aviation. Prices for the aircraft themselves start at around £2,000 for a simple trike going up to around £6,500 for a more advanced three axis machine, but all microlight running costs are low, around £6 per hour.

The cost of the various training courses varies from club to club but the following prices represent the average figures (1983):

Trial flight   £6
One-day introduction course   £28
Five-day solo microlight course   £250

Above *A Tiger Cub pilot prepares for take-off.* **Below** *A Tiger Cub undergoing structural testing during construction.*

Microlight aircraft

For anyone wishing to find out more about individual microlight aircraft, manufacturers will be only too happy to supply further information. The BMAA can help you with addresses and telephone numbers. The following are a cross section of the types of microlights currently on the market, together with basic costs. A number of accessories such as floats for water operation, skis for snow, etc, are available depending on the aircraft type. The cost of learning to fly a microlight is often refundable against the cost of buying your own machine from your school or club (1983 prices):

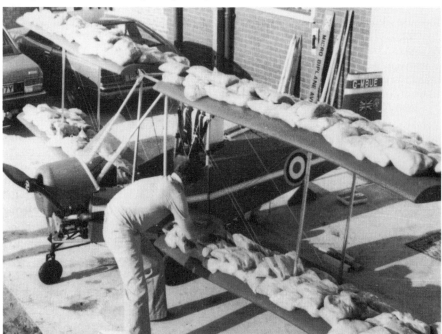

A weight-shift 'trike' preparing for a field landing.

Sky Ranger A two-seat microlight that closely resembles a conventional light aircraft. The pilot and passenger sit side by side in an enclosed cabin with a shared central control stick. It has slow flying speeds and short field landing capabilities and can be folded down for road transportation in its own specially constructed trailer. £6,500 excl VAT.

Lone Ranger As above but a single seater. £4,500 excl VAT.

The Puma The basic concept of the Puma is simple, an efficient hang glider wing supporting a tricycle undercarriage bearing an engine driving a pusher propeller. So it is one with which hang glider pilots will be at home.
£2,194.20 inc VAT.

Tiger Cub A very conventional looking aeroplane just like a small 'Tiger Moth'. The 'Tiger' is a single seater bi-plane powered by a twin cylinder 440 cc Robin engine. With a cruising speed of 60 mph this is the microlight for the person who wishes to fly cross country. £3,578.80 inc VAT.

The Eagle At a first glance this is an odd looking microlight with a wing at the nose and steering carried out by a pair of handlebars. The 'Canard' wing, however, virtually precludes the possibility of stalling and spinning. The 'Eagle' is an extraordinarily safe aircraft to fly—ideal for the beginner. £3,490 inc VAT.

The Mirage This matches the traditional looks of a light aeroplane, the pilot having a traditional control stick, throttle and rudder pedals. £4,174 inc VAT.

The Pathfinder The Pathfinder is a three axis microlight, but also has the simplicity of rigging, de-rigging and portability associated with the most basic trike. The Pathfinder packs down for car top transportation. £3,588 inc VAT.

A student pilot under training in the Eagle microlight.

Tiger Cub 440 production specification

Method of derigging—folding wings.
Rigging time one person less than ten minutes.
Wing span 21 ft 6 in.
Wing area 140 sq ft.
Length 13 ft 9 in.
Height 6 ft.
Wing loading empty (dry) 2 lb per sq ft.
Empty weight (dry) 280 lb (440 cc engine).
Gross weight 535 lb.
Maximum pilot weight 210 lb.

Derigged dimensions

Length 13 ft 6 in.
Height 6 ft.
Width 7 ft 2 in.

Engine

Two-cylinder air-cooled 440 cc 40-50 hp Fuji Robin with H-D single tooth belt drive.

Flight performance

Performance figures quoted at sea level, ambient temperature, 50°F nil wind, runway surface short grass, pilot weight 160 lb. Fuel 5 gallons (imperial). (*NB* Performance figures and specifications are subject to alteration without notice, and the former can vary with any aircraft depending on pilot skill, weight and fuel load. It is the pilot's responsibility to assess air temperature, pressure humidity, surface condition, wind speed, turbulence and wind shear conditions before flying.)
Take off distance less than 40 yds.
Landing distance less than 60 yds.
Rate of climb minimum 700 ft per min.
Recommended cruising speed 60 mph (IAS).
Maximum level speed 80 mph (IAS).
VNE Never exceed speed 85 mph (IAS).
Recommended landing approach speed 45 mph (IAS) (still air).
Recommended gliding speed with engine off, 40 mph.
Mush stall speed with power on, 30 mph.
Operational maximum wind speed (clean air flow) 25 mph.
Operational maximum recommended cross wind component 10 mph.
Rate of roll at 50 mph greater than 30° per second.
Static load tests to $+6g$ $-4g$.

Control

Rudder: pedal operated via 2 mm 7×7 steel wire. *Elevator:* all moving tail plane. Actuated by cockpit centre stick unit coupled by seamless high tensile tube. *Ailerons:* cockpit centre stick operated with differential torsion tube of HT seamless drawn alloy.

Airframe construction

Alloy seamless drawn tube assembled with cadmium plated aircraft quality nuts, bolts, and British Standard Specification HD rivets on secondary structure. Preformed composite flying surfaces Patent No 8214682. Covered with heat shrink woven fabric. Flying wires of steel 2.5 m wire.

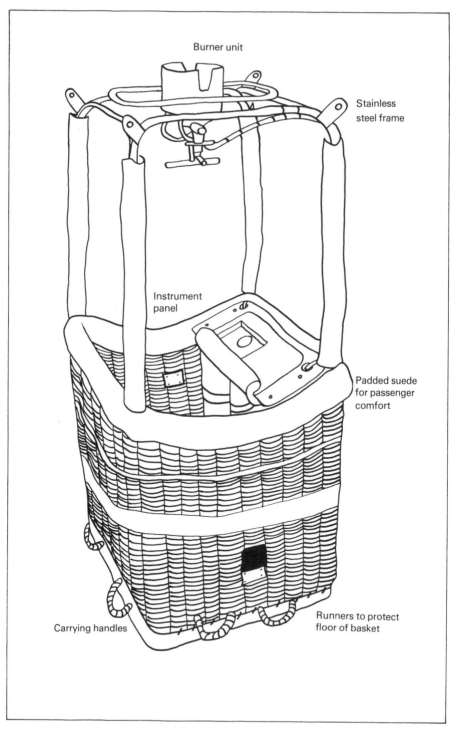

Burner unit

Stainless
steel frame

Instrument
panel

Padded suede
for passenger
comfort

Carrying handles

Runners to protect
floor of basket

A balloon basket.

Chapter 6

Ballooning

There can be few more pleasant ways of experiencing the joys of flying, than a balloon flight over the early morning countryside. The sound of bird song can be clearly heard as the huge nylon balloon drifts slowly over the mist laden fields. The roaring flame of the burner is the only intruder in this silent world.

Modern hot air balloons are large, most are around 1,841 cu m (65,000 cu ft) in capacity and are made of nylon weighing approximately 1.75 oz per sq yd. This material is light yet incredibly strong. When flying has finished for the day, a balloon will fold down to a comparatively small size so it is easily transportable by the family estate car. Because the flame from the burner blasts straight into the open mouth of the balloon, the skirt is usually made of fireproof material such as nomex. The balloon canopy incorporates what is known as a ripping panel and a discharge or dump valve. The ripping panel is a large square of nylon at the very top of the balloon secured by velcro tape around the edges. This provides the pilot on landing, with a means of allowing the hot air to escape quickly, thus deflating the balloon and sparing the crew from an uncomfortable ride along the ground. To prevent the panel being accidentally opened in flight, there is a built-in safety factor. A coloured line has to be broken at three points before the panel can be opened. The discharge valve is located at the side of the balloon canopy, it can be opened or closed in flight to allow excess hot air to escape. It is seldom used as the hot air will have to be replaced later in the flight and propane costs money.

Underneath the canopy is the most important item as far as the crew are concerned, the basket. The basket, and it usually is a genuine woven willow-cane basket, is suspended by stainless steel wire ropes from the skirt of the balloon. As well as providing a cockpit for the crew, it is also home for the burner and various other pieces of auxiliary equipment. The power unit of the balloon works on the same principle as a camping gas stove. The liquid propane gas is vapourised via a coil and passed through a set of four jets to form a flame. The supplies of propane to the main jets from the cylinders are entirely independent, each with its own on/off cock. This is a safety measure as cocks have been known to fail to open when needed. The propane cylinders are usually made of aluminium for lightness and hold approximately 20 kg (44 lb) of liquid propane. The burner is controlled by a single on/off tap connected to the fuel bottles by strong high pressure hoses. The flame is not left on continually, but ignited in bursts approximately 30 seconds apart. These bursts of heat are around the 1,900°C mark and combustion is almost perfect, so there

Left *A Cameron basket and burner unit. The output of the flame can be adjusted from a flicker to a soaring flame.*

Opposite page *Hot air expands the balloon envelope to the size of a house.*

Below *Lambert & Bulter's pair of Thunder Ax6-56zs.*

A Colt balloon with some unusual-looking passengers, taken during the filming of The Great Muppet Caper.

is very little chance of a build up of explosive gases in the balloon canopy. A trail rope of 45 m (150 ft) in length is carried, coiled on the outside of the basket. A dry powder fire extinguisher is also carried.

Constructional details

Balloon canopies are complex. The standard unit is composed of 12 vertical panels or gores, which run from the base to the top of the balloon. The gores are designed to give the balloon its shape and are stitched together with load bearing tapes along the long edges. Each gore panel is made up of 25 sub-panels, each being 3 ft wide and 12 ft long. The overall shape of the finished balloon is derived entirely from the effect of the assembled panels which are increasingly computer designed, therefore care must be taken at the initial cutting stages. A field full of multi-coloured balloons ready for flying is one of the most beautiful sights in aviation. All sorts of different designs can be made using coloured materials for the canopy panels. Most balloon customers have their own ideas for designs and colours and individual manufacturers are happy to supply blank panel diagrams on which the buyer can draw out his own particular scheme. Naturally the more complex the design the more expensive it will be.

Flying the balloon

Sometimes it can be hard to tell when the balloon in which you are about to fly has left the ground. One can be so engrossed in conversation with another crew member, that you have not felt the slight jolt as the balloon lets go its moorings. Before you know it you are rising fast and waving to the toylike figures below. The burner blasts more hot air into the balloon, you keep rising higher and higher, the countryside unfolding like some vast tablecloth below you. You decide to level off at 610 m (2,000 ft) and check to see what the wind is doing.

Visibility is good and you estimate you are drifting to the south. A quick check of your map reveals you are roughly on course. Navigation in good weather is a simple affair, basic map reading being the only skill required. How far you go depends solely on the wind. In the UK it is not often absolutely calm, but it does happen occasionally. If your balloon is becalmed you must wait for the wind to pick up or, by use of the burner, climb higher, where hopefully there may be a drift of wind to transport you on your way. Sometimes, however, the flight will have to end and a landing place selected. A nice green field is picked where the grass looks soft. The pilot can be selective as to his landing place, but only within the confines of his flight path. As the field comes up to meet you, your hand still on the burner controls, the basket gives a slight bump, then another and then you are down. The ripping panel is pulled away and the hot air escapes with a whoosh, the brightly coloured balloon slowly collapses on to the ground around you. With any luck the retrieve crew will be waiting and the packing away can begin. Not all your landings will be on calm days, however. On a

Below left *The Colt Helium Hopper. Due to the high cost of helium, gas balloons have been very few and far between. In fact, this is the first true man-carrying balloon built in Britain since 1952. It has a volume of 150 m³ which gives a gross lift of about 330 lb.*
Below right *The Colt Cloudhopper one-man balloon.*

windy day the landing is much more exciting and you must be prepared for a rough ride. A tight hold on the basket is essential as the balloon may be dragged several hundred feet across a wet and bumpy field.

Learning

It is possible to become a balloon pilot by taking a course of instruction with a commercial school or by joining a syndicate. A typical example is the Europa balloon training school in Essex. Here the instructors are qualified and experienced balloon pilots. A complete course can be taken or it may be split into hourly sessions.

An alternative to learning with a school is to join a syndicate. As with gliding, this is a popular method for several persons to club together to purchase a balloon and share its running costs. If you don't have a ready-made syndicate, contact the editor of the British Balloon and Airship Clubs magazine *The Aerostat*. This means that your name and address can be printed in its pages and other interested persons thinking along the same lines in your part of the country can get in touch with you. If you find it difficult to gather enough

Below left *A Colt large basket.* **Below right** *Propane fuel cylinders.*

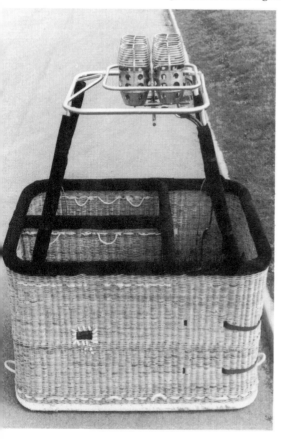 

Inflator fans. These are used to inflate the balloon before the expensive propane gas is used to heat the air inside.

people together, you might try advertising in other aeronautical magazines. The average balloon basket is large enough to carry two or three people and you will pick up a lot of valuable experience whilst flying as a passenger. The smaller the syndicate the better as there will be less people wishing to fly. The bigger the group, more members spending time in the air means less flying for each individual. When you buy a share in a syndicate, remember there will also be maintenance of the trailer and other pieces of ground equipment to be kept in tip top condition.

If you have never flown gliders or light aeroplanes you must develop a healthy respect for the element you are flying in. This is just about the most important thing you have to learn and it is something quite different from knowing how to control your balloon. There are two things you can do to acquire this awareness as quickly as possible.

1 Concentrate 100 per cent on flying when you are in the basket, even when you are not operating the controls. Do not be distracted by people down below and don't be shy about asking your instructor lots of questions.

2 Talk, eat, drink and breathe balloon flying at every available opportunity with those who have more experience than you.

Before your syndicate starts operating as a flying group, it is a good idea to draw up some rules to cover such things as insurance, members' liability for damage to equipment, flying time for each individual member, fees, the sale of the balloon and equipment and resignation of members. It is far better to decide these things in advance and commit them to paper before any situations arise.

Above left *The Thundercolt 'hot airship'.* **Above right** *'If you like a drink while you fly!'*
Opposite page *Thunder Ax7-65 Series 1 carrying a hang glider.*

Licence requirements

To pilot a balloon a Private Pilot's Licence (free balloons hot air) is required
and the following conditions have to be fulfilled.

1 A simplified PPL aeroplane medical examination must be passed, and
should be completed by a CAA approved doctor or the applicant's own GP.

2 The applicant must have made at least six flights totalling 12 hours under
instruction.

3 Take a dual test flight with a CAA approved examiner.

4 Pass three written examinations with a pass mark of at least 70 per cent in
the following subjects: *(a)* Aviation Law and Flight Rules and Procedures; *(b)*
Navigation and Meteorology; *(c)* Aerostatics.

The written examinations are the same as those for a light aircraft pilot, the
additional paper on aerostatics being of a more specialist nature.

Left *Modern hot air balloons can be made in almost any shape, like this one of 'Buzby'.*

Below *British Gas' hot air balloon is launched in Hyde Park at the Great Children's Party in 1979.*

Below right *Thundercolt AS80 hot airship.*

British Balloon and Airship Club

The British Balloon and Airship Club (BBAC) is the national club for British balloon pilots, crew members and enthusiasts. It is recognised as being the representative and governing body for ballooning in the United Kingdom by the Royal Aero Club, the Federation Aeronautique Internationale and the Civil Aviation Authority. The club was founded in 1965 with the following objectives.

1 The formation of an association of persons interested in the practice and encouragement of developing ballooning and airship flying.

2 The encouragement of the study of ballooning and airship flying, pilotage, navigation and improvement of designs of balloons and airships.

3 The holding and arrangement of meetings and competitions in ballooning offering and granting of contributions towards the provision of prizes, awards and distinctions.

4 The promotion of social intercourse between members of the club and their friends.

The club is very active in representing the interests of members in discussions with such organisations as the Civil Aviation Authority (Airworthiness Division and Private Aviation Committee) the conference of general aviation organisations and the Sports Council, to name but a few. At the time of writing, membership fees involve an entry fee of £2 plus annual subscriptions as follows:

junior members under 18 years of age, £2;

full members, £6;

family members, £8.

Entry fee provides a membership package consisting of a cloth badge, club decal, membership card, certificate of membership, lapel pin, membership directory, rules and constitution. Members will receive a bi-monthly copy of the

club's illustrated magazine *The Aerostat*. A pilots' newsletter is circulated to licensed and student pilots. The BBAC organise some of the larger balloon meetings in the UK, many as public spectacle events and some as competitive, including the British Championships which also serves for the selection of a team to represent British ballooning at the world championships.

United Kingdom Civil Aviation Authority
Curriculum for flight training exercises

1 Familiarisation with balloon, equipment and controls.
2 Rigging the balloon for flight.
3 Preparation for flight:
(a) Obtaining met forecast and appreciation of conditions.
(b) Passenger and crew briefing.
(c) Check of down wind hazards.
4 Inflation.
5 Pre take off checks.
6 Take off:
(a) Normal.
(b) Light, from shelter in moderate wind.
7 Level flight, effect of burner.
8 Climbing and descending, use of vent.

9 Approach and overshoot from low level.
10 Use of maps, appreciation of controlled airspace.
11 Landing using vent.
12 Landing using rip panel.
13 Approach and overshoot from high level.
14 Pilot light failure, emergency procedure.
15 Flight in wind greater than 12 knots.
16 Fast climb and descent.
17 Fuel management.
18 Use of trail rope and handling line.
19 Tethered flights.

Airship and balloon system examinations

1 Pre-inflation checks, post inflation checks, crew and passenger briefing, pre-flight checks and in-flight checks.
2 Criteria for take off sites, weather conditions.
3 Launching, in flight and landing hazards and precautions, problems of immediate touch downs.
4 Flying in convection, hazards and precautions.
5 Landing criteria for landing fields, crowd control, relationship with landowners.
6 Emergency procedures in the event of failure of burner system or pilot system.

Premature descents in down draughts. Miscalculation of take off angle or approach glide path. Emergency use of burner, ripping line, ballast and trail rope.
7 Canopy controls definition and purpose of primary and secondary elements permissible damage.
8 Propane, properties in liquid and gaseous form. Ground handling and transfer. Storage and fire prevention, laws and regulations.
9 Burners—principles of operation, main elements and controls, output in different ambient conditions, care and maintenance.

Ballooning Code of Practice

The British Balloon and Airship Club is well aware of the necessity for maintaining good public relations with farmers and other landowners. Like the British Gliding Association and the British Hang Gliding Association, it has drawn up a code of conduct with the National Farmers' Union for the guidance of its members. A copy of this code is issued to all balloon pilots and crewmen. The following rules are included:

Flight planning

Do not fly unless you are reasonably certain that your flight path will be over country which is suitable for a balloon to land. For example during the summer months you should avoid flying over standing crops, particularly corn in light wind conditions.

Taking off

Always obtain permission from the farmer or landowner before driving your equipment on to the field. Check, during the climb out immediately down wind of the take off site, that the balloon's flight path will not overfly livestock. Brief all groundcrew and other helpers to make sure gates are closed after use.

In the air

Always fly at a height such that you do not deliberately cause any disturbance to livestock by flying within (152 m (500 ft) of them. If it looks as though the animals have been disturbed for any reason note the location of the incident and check the cause with the farmer after landing. If you cannot locate the farmer, inform the local police.

The landing and retrieval

Select a field that should cause the least possible inconvenience to the farmer, landowner or other members of the public. Particular care must be taken during the summer months when standing crops cover large areas of the countryside. Remember the risk of fire during this period can be great.

Before deploying the trail rope check that the ground ahead and below is clear of power lines, buildings and livestock. When the balloon has landed discourage onlookers from entering the field and trespassing on the farmer's property. Contact the farmer or landowner as soon as possible after landing. Obtain permission to bring recovery vehicles onto the land.

Never make tethered flights or re-inflate the balloon in the landing field unless you have obtained permission to do so from the farmer or landowner.

If the farmer or landowner cannot be contacted after landing, you must try to obtain his address and contact him as soon as possible afterwards. If damage is caused or the farmer wishes to take further action exchange names and addresses, including that of your insurers.

Standard balloon classes

International Class	Capacity (cu ft)	(m³)	Crew	Operations
AX3	20,000	566	1	Minimum manned hot air balloon. Pilot flies in harness. Not for beginners.
AX4	31,000	890	1	One man balloon with full flight capacity.
AX5	42,000	1,190	1-2	Two man balloon, also ideal for longer solo flights.
AX6	56,000	1,590	2-3	Convenient to operate but a bit small for club flying.
AX7	65,000	1,840	3	Good size for clubs.
AX7	77,000	2,180	3-4	Good size for clubs.
AX8	84,000	2,380	4	
AX8	105,000	2,970	6	Good for long duration and high altitude flight.
AX9	140,000	3,935	8	Also very suitable for hot countries.

Hot air airships

The shape of ballooning has changed recently and craft known as hot air airships have begun to appear. Instead of the balloon envelope being bulbous, it is cigar shaped, nearly 30 m (100 ft) in length and requiring over 2,688 cu m (96,000 cu ft) of hot air for inflation. These craft, as well as rising with the help of a burner, have forward motion thanks to a small 1,600 cc engine driving a pusher propeller.

Instead of a basket these airships usually have a light fibre-glass gondola amidships carrying a crew of two. As a practical means of transport they are not really effective with a cruising speed of only 20-25 knots. But just for pleasure use, three or four syndicate members could have an enjoyable time flying one.

A Cameron balloon prepares for lift-off.

The one-man Colt Cloudhopper lands on a skyscraper in Mexico City. The ballooning sequence is the main stunt in the film Green Ice.

Ballooning—Glossary of terms

Bullet A metal peg attached to the top of the rip line.

Burn To turn on the on/off control and allow the main burner to burn at full power.

Burner The unit consisting of the coiled stainless steel tubing that feeds the propane fuel to the jets.

Car lines Stainless steel wires running around and under the basket and emerging at the top, extending upwards and attached to the underside of the burner offload ring.

Copybook landing A perfect landing, without tipping the basket over and with the minimum of vertical speed.

Crew chief The senior ground crew member who is responsible for the inflation and launching of the balloon.

Crown Top of the balloon.

Crown line A strong line attached to the top or crown of the balloon and used to hold it down during inflation.

Dog house landing A very fast landing which results in the balloon basket turning upside down.

Dump To open the dump valve in order to lose hot air and thus height.

Dump line The line made of stainless steel wire attached to the dump valve or window and running down to the cockpit.

Dump valve A fabric window which can be opened by means of the dump line to allow sufficient hot air to escape to allow the balloon to descend.

Envelope The balloon canopy.

False lift When the balloon lifts off and starts to climb and then begins to descend again. This is usually due to incorrect weighing off or being assisted off the ground by enthusiastic but unskilled helpers.

Good landing A landing that you can walk away from.

Handling line A thin rope line approximately 61 m (200 ft) in length.

Hands off During the 'hands off' helpers stand around the balloon basket firmly holding it on the ground. In order to tell whether the balloon has enough lift to rise from the ground all helpers raise their hands vertically above the basket. If the balloon is ready for flight the basket will rise and the order 'hands on' can be given. When the pilot is ready for lift off he will say 'hands off and stand back'.

Heavy When the air in the balloon is not hot enough to keep it in equilibrium and the balloon starts to descend.

Light When the balloon is ready to leave the ground or is ascending.

Load ring The metal surround which holds the burner unit suspended by the rigging lines beneath the mouth of the balloon.

Mouth The bottom open part of the balloon.

Pilot light A small pipe and jet which enables a constant flame to be available for re-igniting the main burner.

Rigging lines Stainless steel wires running from load tapes to the burner ring.

Rip To pull open the rip panel to deflate the balloon.

Rip line A line attached to the top of the rip panel and running down to the balloon basket.

Rip panel Large triangular section of a balloon canopy laced or fixed in place with velcro tape, which can be pulled open to deflate the balloon.

Skirt Fire resistant material hung around the mouth of the balloon to assist inflation.

Tie off thread Breaking thread, 14 kg (30 lb), used to secure rip.

Vigorous landing A term used by a pilot who has come in to land far too fast and the balloon has bounced back into the air before coming to rest.

Weighing off Checking for positive lift ie, making sure the balloon will fly when hands off command is given.

Work person All helpers and ground crew other than the pilot and crew chief.

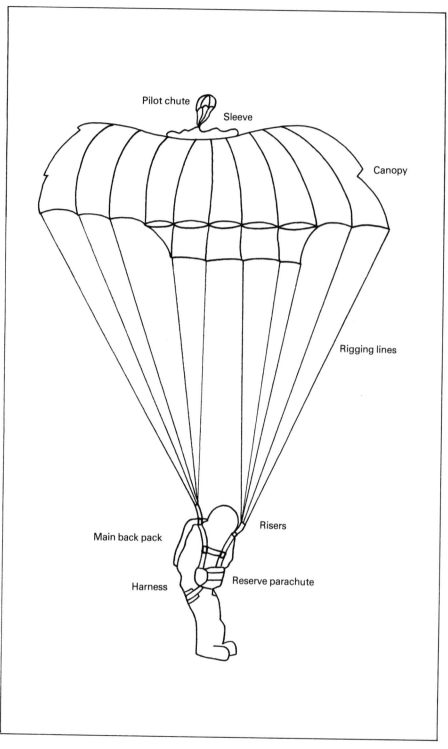

Pilot chute

Sleeve

Canopy

Rigging lines

Risers

Main back pack

Harness

Reserve parachute

Chapter 7

Parachuting

The modern parachute has its origins firmly in the military, where it was developed as a means of escaping from a balloon or, later, a disabled aircraft in flight. The sport parachute has seen tremendous research and design work in the last two decades thanks to the work of NASA and the US space programme, where parachutes were used to land returning Gemini and Apollo spacecraft into the sea. The considerable knowledge acquired about aerodynamic deceleration will no doubt be reflected in future parachute designs and techniques generally.

For competition parachuting the canopy needs to be steerable to enable pin-point landings on a 10 cm (4 in) disc to be made. The development of steerable accuracy means that parachute canopies are no longer at the mercy of the wind. With a modern parachute such as the para commander, the vents at the rear of the canopy give it a wing-like quality and impart a gliding motion as it moves forward through the air. A bonus of this type of design is that it reduces the landing speed and the expert can alight on his feet with a stand up arrival every

Opposite page *Parachute composition.* **Below** *The first scientific approach to parachute design is to be found in the sketches of Leonardo Da Vinci (1452-1519).*

time. Another major development in parachute design has been the incorporation of the sleeve, which assists deployment of the rigging lines and canopy, much reducing the risk of fouling by the parachutist. This design work and incorporation of safety features has done much to contribute to the excellent record of safety enjoyed by the sport. However, it is still a legal requirement in the United Kingdom, that the sport parachutist carries a smaller reserve parachute on all jumps.

The advent in recent years of large numbers of military and civil display teams, has brought sport parachuting to the public eye. Thanks to the popular press it is not unknown for everyday folk to take part in fund-raising first jumps for charity. These are well publicised and contribute to a good cause. Also thanks to this public awareness, more and more people are taking up sport parachuting as a fascinating hobby.

Is it for you?

This is the question every would-be parachutist must ask him or herself. When you are thousands of feet up in the sky and about to throw yourself into the emptiness of space, it is no time to have any self doubts. This sport calls for confidence, both in oneself and in the training your instructor has given you. The controlling body of the sport in the United Kingdom is the British Parachute Association, Kimberley House, Vaughn Way, Leicester LE1 4SG. This association is responsible to the Civil Aviation Authority for the training and safety standards of all parachutists military and civilian alike. All parachutists are required to observe the strict rules laid down for their safety and the safety of others. The current membership of the association is in excess of 21,000 and more than 79,000 parachutists have joined since its formation in 1962. There are approximately 12 full-time and 28 part-time clubs at the time of writing. A number of service clubs and associations also exist in the United Kingdom, Cyprus, Germany and Hong Kong. In Scotland, which has its own Scottish Parachute Association, there are currently four clubs in operation.

A full list of parachute schools and clubs can be found in Appendix 7. The minimum age for sport parachuting is 16. The consent of a parent/guardian is required for those under the age of 18. All persons joining a parachuting course will be required to complete a declaration of fitness to jump, stating that they have never suffered from any of the following: epilepsy, fits, recurrent fainting, giddiness or blackouts, unusually high blood pressure, a previous coronary thrombosis (myocardinal infarction), diabetes in any form or schizophrenia. In addition to the medical conditions listed above, the following may cause difficulty whilst parachuting and if you suffer from or have suffered from any of these, you are advised to take medical advice: chronic bronchitis, severe asthma, pneumathorax, rheumatic fever, any chronic disorder of bone or joints, severe anaemia, previous major head injury, chronic ear or sinus disease. With regard to eyesight, vision of 6/12 with or without correction in one eye is acceptable, provided that the eye has normal visual field. It is therefore permissible for someone to jump who has vision, although defective, in one eye only.

You should not parachute if you are on medication of any kind. Students are also advised that during instruction and parachuting activities the consumption of alcohol is forbidden. You will be expected to join the British Parachute Association, membership of which includes third party public liability cover up

BRITISH PARACHUTE ASSOCIATION
KIMBERLEY HOUSE
47 VAUGHN WAY
LEICESTER
Tel Leicester (0533) 59778/55635

DECLARATION OF FITNESS TO PARACHUTE

I HEREBY DECLARE that I have never suffered from any of the following conditions which may create or lead to a dangerous situation during parachuting with regard to myself and with regard to other persons . . .

EPILEPSY FITS, RECURRENT FAINTING, GIDDYNESS OR BLACKOUTS, UNUSUALLY HIGH BLOOD PRESSURE, A PREVIOUS CORONARY THROMBOSIS (MYOCARDIAL INFARCTION), DIABETES IN ANY FORM, SCHIZOPHRENIA.

I FURTHER DECLARE that, in the event of my contracting, or suspecting any of the above conditions in the future, I will cease to parachute until I have obtained medical opinion.

_____   _____

Parachutist's name in CAPITALS   Parachutist's Signature

_____   Date _____

Signature of WITNESS—in the case of a minor (under 18 years) this must be the signature of the PARENT/GUARDIAN

IF BECAUSE OF ANY OF THE ABOVE QUOTED CONDITIONS, YOU CANNOT SIGN THE ABOVE FORM OR IF YOU ARE OVER THE AGE OF FORTY, YOU MUST, BEFORE PARACHUTING, OBTAIN THE SIGNATURE OF A DOCTOR.

DOCTOR'S CERTIFICATE

I understand that the applicant wishes to parachute but has been unable to sign the above declaration. In my opinion, it is safe for him/her to do so.

_____

Doctor's Signature

DOCTOR'S STAMP

Date _____

In case of doubt, the Medical Examiner to the British Parachute Association will be pleased to advise and may be contacted at the address on the top of this form.

The declaration of fitness called for by the British Parachute Association.

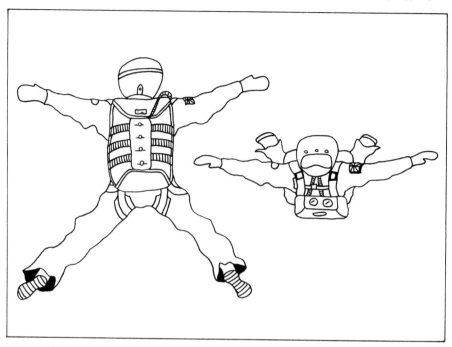

The 'stable spread' position. The static line student will learn this position in basic training which will ensure he or she always falls to earth face-first.

to £250,000 for any one incident. When you join the BPA you will receive a subscription to the bi-monthly magazine *The Sport Parachutist.* You should only join the BPA when you have made contact with a club who will supply all the necessary forms.

Ground training

Assuming you have made up your mind, you turn up at the club for a course of instruction. A weekend course of parachuting instruction at the time of writing (1983) costs around £49. This includes insurance, hire of equipment, instructional and administrative costs, the first descent and one year's club membership. Subsequent descents cost approximately £6 each parachute supplied. The student must make a minimum of six descents using automatically opened parachutes before he will be allowed to operate his own ripcord. Before you begin training, you will need the proper clothing and equipment. At most clubs you will be expected to provide a helmet (an open faced motor cycle type will do), a light coloured jump suit or tracksuit and boots. Some clubs will hire or lend you a helmet and suit for your first jump, individual clubs will be happy to supply further details. The type of place used for parachute training is often little more than a grass field, a take off strip for the aircraft and one or two hangars. If one has good weather for the initial training, most instruction will be carried on out of doors. You will be given lectures and practical training in subjects such as safety regulations, parachute packing and aircraft exit procedures.

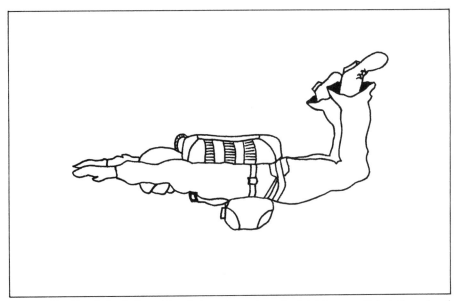

Above *The 'frog' freefall position is less tiring than the 'stable spread' but the rate of descent is faster.* **Below** *Pulling the ripcord.*

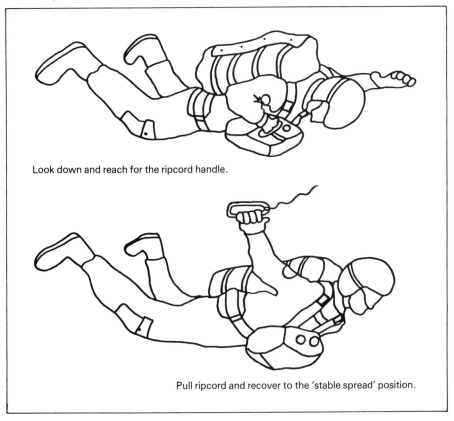

Look down and reach for the ripcord handle.

Pull ripcord and recover to the 'stable spread' position.

The full training programme as recommended by the British Parachute Association is as follows:

A Orientation

1 Documentation, check restricted permit, BPA classification card, etc.
2 Outline of the training syllabus.
3 Routine safety instructions to be observed with aircraft.
4 Orientation flight.

B Introduction

1 Safety regulations.
2 Equipment and clothing.
3 Introduction to aircraft type in use.
4 Determination of wind drift.
5 Exit technique (stability).
6 Emergency procedures.
7 Canopy handling.
8 Landing techniques.
9 Parachute packing.

C Familiarisation with parachutes

1 The anatomy of the main assembly.
2 The anatomy of the reserve assembly.
3 The functioning of main and reserve parachutes.
4 Parachute fitting.
5 Pre-planning a parachute descent.
6 Equipment checking procedure.

D The jumping aircraft

1 Safety checks.
2 Procedures for entering and exiting the aircraft.
3 Static line procedure.
4 Signals and words of command in the air.

E Aircraft exits

1 Commands, signals and actions.
2 Move into exit position.
3 Position after exit (stable position).
4 Counting, count follow through and ripcord procedure.

F Emergency procedures

1 Verbal count static line.
2 Verbal count free fall.

3 Check of main canopy immediately after opening.
4 Recognition of malfunction.
5 Corrective action.
6 Drill period using suspended harness.

G Canopy handling

1 Checking canopy.
2 Orientation with the ground:
(a) Grasp toggles.
(b) Check location over target and drift.
(c) Work to wind (zig zag method).
(d) Check vertical angle of descent.
(e) Avoidance of obstacles.
(f) Harness drill period.

H Preparing to land

1 Attitude to adopt landing position.
2 Body position face into wind.
3 Obeying ground instructions.

I Parachute landing falls

1 Normal.
2 Tree.
3 Power line.
4 Water.
5 Points of body contact.

J Field packing the parachute

1 Chain lines.
2 Sleeve over canopy.
3 Close one side flap with side opening bands.
4 Secure all equipment and go to parachute packing area.

K Drop zone

1 Responsibility.
2 Control.
3 Rotation of ground personnel.

L Parachute packing instruction

Backpacks only.

M Testing all phases

This is the British Parachute Association recommended training schedule. Its aim is to turn you into a safe and competent parachutist. During the parachute packing phase, backpacks only will be packed, reserves are only packed by instructors and other qualified people.

 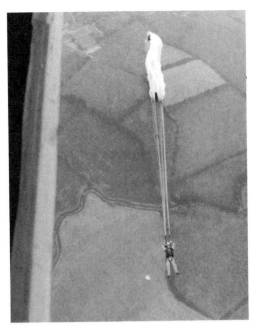

Above left *A student parachutist falls away on his first jump.* **Above right** *The parachute deploys after a static line drop.* **Below left** *The 'Double L' basic parachute.* **Below right** *This position is not quite right. It is a first jump, however, and will improve with practice.*

Above left *'Thumbs up', the long free fall to earth begins.* **Above right** *The arched position ensures a free fall.*

The aircraft

If you have ever watched a military display team such as the Army 'Red Devils' or RAF 'Falcons' run and throw themselves into space from the ramp of a Hercules transport, forget it. The aircraft you will almost certainly use will be the Cessna 172. It is a four-seat light aircraft with a high set wing and a fixed undercarriage. This aeroplane will be the parachute club's property or hired from the local flying club; its great advantage is its ability to fly at the low speeds at which parachuting takes place. With the passenger seats removed and the starboard door taken off, a small steel step is fitted over the wheel and we have our jumping aircraft.

The Cessna 172 can lift three parachutists plus pilot, and if fuel costs are to be kept down must waste no time in reaching the required height and returning to land. In the hands of a skilled pilot the aircraft is likely to be back on the ground before the parachutists. Its larger brother the Cessna 182, can lift four jumpers plus pilot. If you are lucky enough to train at a certain club near Peterborough, your jump aircraft may be the Pilatus PC-6 Turboporter. This aircraft is turbine powered and capable of lifting eight parachutists plus two crew.

Above *Adopting the 'stable spread' position on exit from the jump step of a Cessna.*
Below *Step jump used on the Cessna 172/180/182 series aircraft.*

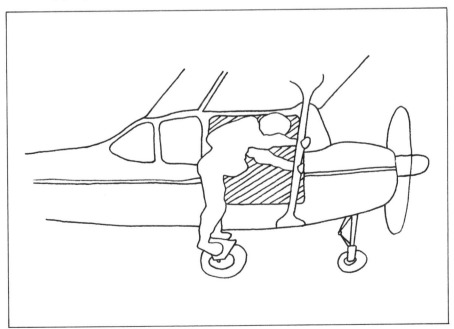

Jumping

The first half a dozen jumps that you make will be with a static line. This eliminates the need to pull a ripcord. When you step off the wheel of the Cessna you will fall to the full length of the static line, about 5 m (15 ft). As the line is pulled tight it will snap out the pins of your backpack and the drogue or pilot chute will pull the sleeve into the air. The main canopy will then deploy and there you are, floating high above the earth beneath your nylon umbrella. To assist the canopy to open safely, you should assume the full spread, or stable position on leaving the aircraft. This will ensure that you do not spin and thus entangle your rigging lines, a most unpleasant situation. When you fall you will begin to count, the standard count is: 1,000 2,000 3,000 4,000 check canopy. If the main parachute canopy has not opened by this time the reserve parachute must be deployed. This smaller reserve chute is approximately 7 m (24 ft) in diameter and bearing a 91 kg (200 lb) parachutist will stabilise the rate of fall to roughly 8 m (25 ft) per second. The reserve pack has no drogue chute, so deploys more rapidly and saves vital seconds in an emergency. This counting is critical, especially in freefall parachuting.

After you have made a minimum of six descents with a static line, you will be allowed to open the parachute yourself. As you gain more experience, you will delay opening your parachute for longer and longer drops. If you leave your jump aircraft at a height of 3,660 m (12,000 ft) you will be able to free fall for 60 seconds. This is about the most practicable height from which to jump without using oxygen.

When you are a more experienced parachutist, you may wish to enter competitions. There are three main specialisations in competition jumping:

Accuracy On an accuracy jump the object is to land on a 10 cm (4 in) disc in the centre of a gravel pit. When dead centre is the aim, style comes second and the jumper concerns himself only with getting his heel as close as possible to the target.

Style On a style jump the parachutist has to perform a series of international manoeuvres during free fall, examples are a 360 degree turn and forward loop.

Relative In star or relative work, parachutists combine in free fall to form patterns and link ups, plunging earthwards at 193 km/h (120 mph) before dispersing to open their canopies.

Grades of competence

No parachutist's licences are required by the British Parachute Association, instead a series of grades of competence are available. These are as follows:

Category 1 Has been passed out on basic ground training (a total of six hours) and is ready for first static line descent.

Category 2 Has performed a minimum of three absolutely stable observed static line descents in the full spread position, counting throughout; has completed a total of 13 hours of ground training in accordance with BPA minimum ground training programme.

Category 3 Has performed a minimum of three successful and consecutive observed static line descents with dummy pulls (counting throughout).

Category 4 (5 seconds) Has performed a minimum of five stable 5 second delayed openings (counting throughout); has remained stable throughout opening on each descent; has looked at ripcord handle before and during the 'reach and pull'; has achieved reasonable canopy handling.

Above *Lined up into wind, a 'para-commander' prepares for landing.*

Above right *The small drogue chute can be seen clearly here.*

Right *The landing position, knees bent, elbows tucked in ready for the touch-down.*

These skydivers are making an intentional water jump, hence the need for life-jackets.

Category 5 (10 seconds) Has performed a minimum of five stable 10 second delayed openings (counting throughout); has learned to maintain heading during exit and in free fall.

Category 6 (15 seconds) Has performed a minimum of five stable 15 second delayed openings in the following sequence: (a) two flat stable; (b) after instruction in the use of instruments three flat stable descents using instruments but continuing to count throughout. After successful completion of the above, has demonstrated the ability to perform 360 degree turns in each direction, stopping on the aircraft heading.

Category 7 (20 seconds) Has performed a minimum of five stable 20 second delayed openings, has demonstrated the ability to recover from an unstable position leaving the aircraft; has been introduced to spotting.

Category 8 (20 seconds) Has landed within 46 m (50 yds) of centre of target on a minimum of three 30 second delayed opening descents; has learned to track and turn in a track; has been cleared for self spotting descents up to 2,135 m (7,000 ft).

Category 9 Has demonstrated to an instructor in free fall that he is fully in control of his movements, is aware of other parachutists around him/her and is capable of taking avoiding action; has demonstrated the ability to perform forward loops, backward loops and barrel rolls; has been introduced to relative parachuting.

Category 10 Has demonstrated his/her ability for unsupervised relative work, having successfully executed the following: (a) the ability to perform a link, followed by a backloop and a second link with another category 10 parachutist approved by the Chief Instructor on a single jump; (b) the ability to close third on a three man group on two separate occasions; (c) he/she has been cleared for self spotted descents up to 3,660 m (12,000 ft).

Note Up to and including category 6, all parachute students are observed and timed from exiting the aircraft until full canopy deployment, by the jumpmaster in the aircraft.

FAI British Standard Certificates Issued by The Royal Aero Club of the United Kingdom

'A' Certificate—Category 3: 10 jumps.

'B' Certificate—Category 5: 25 jumps, to include 10 jumps landing within 50 m (164 ft) of the target.

'C' Certificate—Category 8: 50 jumps, to include 20 jumps landing within 20 m (66 ft) of the target.

'D' Certificate—Category 10: 200 free fall jumps, to include 20 jumps landing within 15 m (49 ft) of the target.

Appendices

1   Where to fly

Avon

Bristol & Wessex Aeroplane Club
Lulsgate Airport
Bristol, Avon
PPL, IMC, Night, Multi, R/T

Bedfordshire

Rogers Aviation Ltd
Cranfield Airfield
*PPL, RT, IMC, Multi, Night, IR, FIC,
CPL, ATPL, GS*

Trent Air Services
Cranfield Airfield
*PPL, R/T, IMC, Night, Multi,
Aerobatics, PPL (H), CPL (H), ATPL,
GS*

Berkshire

West London Aero Club
White Waltham Airfield
Maidenhead
PPL, IR, Multi, Night, Aerobatics

Buckinghamshire

Denham Flying Training School Ltd
Denham Aerodrome, Denham
PPL, R/T, Simulator

Wycombe Air Centre Ltd
Wycombe Air Park
Booker
*PPL, R/T, IMC, Multi, Night, FIC,
AFIC*

Cambridgeshire

Peterborough Aero Club
Sibson Airfield
Peterborough
PPL, R/T, IMC, Night

Rural Flying Corps Ltd
Bourne Aerodrome
Cambridge
*PPL, R/T, IMC, Multi, Night, Tailwheel
conversions, Radio nav*

Cheshire

Manchester School of Flying
Manchester Airport
PPL, R/T, IMC, Multi, Night, IR

Cornwall

Cornwall Flying Club
Bodmin Airfield
PPL, R/T, IMC, Night, Aerobatics

Lands End Flying Club
Lands End Aerodrome
Penzance
PPL, IMC

Derbyshire

Donair Flying Club
East Midlands Airport
PPL, R/T, IMC, Night

East Midlands School of Flying
East Midlands Airport
*PPL, R/T, IMC, Night, Multi, FIC,
Aerobatics*

Devon

Dunkeswell Aero Club
Dunkeswell Airport
Honiton
PPL, R/T, IMC, Night, Multi, Link

Exeter Flying Club
Exeter Airport
PPL, R/T, IMC, Night, AFIC

Dorset

Bournemouth Flying Club
Hurn Airport
PPL, R/T, IMC, Night

Co Durham

Cleveland Flying School
Teesside Airport
PPL, R/T, IMC, Night, Multi

Teesside Flying School
Teesside Airport
PPL, IMC, Night

Essex

Helicopter Hire Ltd
Southend Airport
PPL, H

Stapleford Flight Centre
Stapleford Aerodrome
Romford
*PPL, R/T, IMC, Night, Multi, FIC,
AFIC, IR, Aerobatics, Simulator*

Gloucestershire

Cotswold Aero Club
Staverton Airport
PPL, IMC, Night

Severn Valley Flying Club
Staverton Airport
PPL, IMC, Multi, Night

Hampshire

South Coast Aero Club
Southampton Airport
PPL, R/T, IMC, Multi, Night, Radio nav

Western Air Training Ltd
Thruxton Airfield
Andover
PPL, R/T, IMC, Night

Herefordshire

Herefordshire Aero Club Ltd
Shobden Airfield
Leominster
PPL, R/T, IMC, Night, Aerobatics, Link

Hertfordshire

London School of Flying
Elstree Aerodrome
*PPL, R/T, IMC, Night, Multi, IR,
Simulator, Radio nav*

Humberside

Solo Flying School & Club Ltd
Humberside Airport
*PPL, R/T, IMC, Night, Multi, AFIC,
Aerobatics, Aero instructor*

Isle of Wight

Isle of Wight Flying Club & School
Sandown Airport
PPL, R/T, IMC

Kent

Air Touring Club Ltd
Biggin Hill Airport
Biggin Hill
PPL, R/T, IMC, Night

Headcorn Flying School
Headcorn Aerodrome
Also at Rochester Airport
PPL, R/T, IMC, Night, Radio nav

King Air Flying Club
Biggin Hill Airport
Biggin Hill
*PPL, IMC, Night, IR, Multi, AFIC,
Aerobatics, Radio nav*

Lancashire

ANT Flying Club
Blackpool Airport
PPL, R/T, IMC, Night, Multi, FIC

Lancashire Aero Club
Barton Aerodrome
Eccles
PPL, IMC, Night, AFIC, Aerobatics

Liverpool Aero Club & Flying School
Liverpool Airport
PPL, R/T, IMC, Night, Multi

Woodvale Aero Club
RAF Woodvale
PPL, IMC

Leicestershire

Leicestershire Aero Club Ltd
Leicestershire Airport
*PPL, IMC, Night, FIC, AOPA, Radio
nav, Aerobatics*

Lincolnshire

Fenland Flight Centre
Holbeach St John's Airfield
PPL, IMC, Night

Skegness Aero Club
Skegness Aerodrome
*PPL, IMC, AOPA Radio nav, Tailwheel
conversion*

Wickenby Flying Club Ltd
Wickenby Airfield
Langworth
PPL, R/T, IMC, Aerobatics

Norfolk

Felthorpe Flying Group Ltd
Felthorpe Airfield
No ab initio *training, Tailwheel conversions, Aerobatics*

Norfolk & Norwich Aero Club
RAF Swanton Morley
Dereham
PPL, R/T, IMC, Night

Northamptonshire

Northampton School of Flying
Sywell Airport
PPL, R/T, IMC, Night, Aerobatics

Nottinghamshire

Sheffield Aero Club
Netherthorpe Aerodrome
PPL, R/T, IMC, Simulator

Oxfordshire

Oxford Air Training School
Oxford Airport
PPL, R/T, IMC, Night, Multi, AFIC, Aerobatics, Nav aids course, Commercial IR 1179

Shropshire

Shropshire Aero Club
Sleap Aerodrome
Myddle
PPL, IMC, Night, Aerobatics, FIC

Suffolk

Horizon Flying Club
Ipswich Airport
PPL, IMC, Night, Aerobatics, AOPA, Radio nav

Ipswich School of Flying
Ipswich Airport
PPL, R/T, IMC, Night

Suffolk Aero Club
Ipswich Airport
PPL, IMC, Night, AFIC, Aerobatics, Formation

Surrey

Three Counties Aero Club
Blackbushe Airport
PPL, R/T, IMC, Night, Aerobatics FIC, Simulator

The Mooney Turbo 231 on left with a model 201 on right.

Sussex

Air South Flying Group
Shoreham Airport
*PPL, IMC, Night, Multi, Tailwheel
conversions*

Toon Ghose Aviation
Shoreham Airport
PPL, R/T, IMC, Multi

Tyne & Wear

Newcastle Upon Tyne Aero Club
Newcastle Airport
PPL, R/T, IMC, Night

Sunderland Flying Club
Sunderland Aerodrome
*PPL, R/T, IMC, Night, Multi,
Aerobatics*

Warwickshire

Coventry Aeroplane Club
Coventry Airport
PPL, Night, IMC

F R Aviation Ltd Flying School
Coventry Airport
PPL, IMC, Night

Smith School of Flying
Wellesbourne Mountford Aerodrome
PPL, R/T, IMC, Night, Multi, Radio nav

West Midlands

Executive Air Flying School
Birmingham Airport
PPL, R/T, IMC, Night

Midland Aviation Centre
Halfpenny Green Airport
Bobbington
PPL, R/T, IMC

Wiltshire

Air Compton Ltd
Compton Abbas Airfield
Ashmore
*PPL, R/T, IMC, Multi, AFIC,
Aerobatics*

Yorkshire

Doncaster Aero Club Ltd
Doncaster Airport
*PPL, R/T, IMC, Night, AFIC,
Aerobatics*

Sherburn Aero Club Ltd
Sherburn in Elmet Aerodrome
Leeds
PPL, R/T, IMC, AOPA nav

Yorkshire Aeroplane Club
Leeds/Bradford Airport
*PPL, IMC, Night, Multi, FIC,
Aerobatics*

1980 model Piper Saratoga.

Channel Islands

Channel Aviation
States Airport
Guernsey
PPL, IMC, Night, IR, AOPA, Radio nav

Channel Islands Aero Club
Jersey Airport
PPL, R/T, IMC, Night, Aerobatics

Isle of Man

Lewis Flying Club
Ronaldsway Airport
PPL, IMC, Night

Manx Flyers Aero Club
Ronaldsway Airport
PPL, R/T, IMC, Night, Radio nav

Northern Ireland

Eglinton Flying Club
Eglinton Airfield
Londonderry
PPL, R/T, IMC

Woodgate Aviation Flying School
Belfast Airport
PPL, R/T, IMC, IR, Multi, FIC, Night

Ulster Flying Club
Portaferry Road
Newtownards
PPL, IMC, Night

Woodgate Aviation (St Angelo)
St Angelo Airport
Enniskillen
County Fermanagh
PPL, R/T, IMC, Multi, Night

Scotland

Couger Flying Group
Prestwick Airport
PPL, IMC, Night, Multi

Edinburgh Flying Club Ltd
Edinburgh Airport
PPL, IMC, Night

Glasgow Flying Club Ltd
Glasgow Airport
PPL, IMC, Night, Multi

Highland Aero Club
Dalcross Airport
Inverness
PPL, R/T, IMC, Night, Aerobatics, Radio nav

Prestwick Flying Group
Prestwick Airport
PPL, R/T, IMC, Night, Aerobatics

Shetland Flying Club
Tingwell Aerodrome
PPL, R/T, IMC, Night

Tayside Flying Club
Dundee Airport
PPL, IMC, Night

West of Scotland Flying Club
Glasgow Airport
PPL, IMC, Night, Multi

Wales

Cambrian Flying Club
Cardiff-Wales Airport
PPL, R/T, IMC, Multi, Night, AFIC, AOPA, Radio nav, Aerobatics

Mona Flying Club
RAF Mona
Anglesey
PPL, R/T, IMC, Night, AOPA, Radio nav

North Wales Flying Centre
Caernarfon Airfield
PPL, R/T, IMC, Night, Multi

Simulators

Air Training Services Ltd
38/40 Vanston Place
London SW6 1AX
PPL, R/T, IMC, IR, IF, Radio nav, Technicals & examinations

Flytsim Training Ltd
Bell Street
Maidenhead
Berks
PPL/IR, CPL/IR

Simulated Flight Training
Hurn Airport
Dorset
PPL/IMC, PPL/IR, CPL/IR, RT (VHF & HF) 1179

2   Where to helicopter

Alan Mann Helicopters Ltd
Fairoaks Airfield
Chobham
Surrey
PPL H, IR rating, Turbine rating

Gleneagle Helicopters
Edinburgh Airport
Edinburgh
Scotland
PPL H

Helicopter Hire Ltd
Southend Airport
Southend
Essex
PPL H

March Helicopters Ltd
Sywell Aerodrome
Northants
PPL H, Turbine rating

Norman Bailey Helicopters Ltd
Eastleigh Airport
Southampton
Hants
PPL H, AFI (H), Night rating

Oxford Air Training School
Oxford Airport
Oxfordshire
PPL H, CPL H, Turbine rating

Skyline Helicopters Ltd
The Helipad
Wycombe Air Park
Bucks
PPL H, Turbine rating

Southenair
Shoreham Airport
Shoreham
Sussex
PPL H, Turbine rating

Trent Air Services
Cranfield Airfield
Bedfordshire
*PPL H, CPL H, ATLP, IR rating,
Turbine rating, Instructor rating*

SA 341 Gazelle hovering at the standard height of 3 ft at the Westland Heliport at Battersea.

3   Where to glide

London & the South-East

Essex Gliding Club
North Weald Airfield
Bassett
Nr Epping
Essex

Kent Gliding Club
Squids Gate
Challock
Nr Ashford
Kent

London Gliding Club
Dunstable Downs
Tring Road
Dunstable
Bedfordshire

Ridgewell Oatley Gliding Club
Ridgewell Airfield
Essex

Thames Valley Gliding Club
Wycombe Air Park
Booker
Nr Marlow
Bucks

Tiger Club Soaring Group
Redhill Aerodrome
Redhill
Surrey

Wycombe Gliding School
Booker Airfield
Nr Marlow
Bucks

South & West

Albatross Gliding Club
Davidstow Airfield
Nr Camelford
Cornwall

Bath & Wiltshire Gliding Club
Keevil Aerodrome
Keevil
Wiltshire

Cornwall Gliding Club
Trevellas Airfield
Perranporth
Cornwall

Devon & Somerset Gliding Club
North Hill Airfield
Broadhembury
Honiton
Devon

Dorset Gliding Club
Tarrent Rushton Airfield
Blandford Forum
Dorset

Dunkeswell Gliding Club
Dunkeswell Airfield
Nr Honiton
Devon

East Sussex Gliding Club
Upper Broyle Farm
Broyle
Ringmer
Sussex

Glamorgan Gliding Club
83 Brytirion Hill
Bridgend
Glamorgan

Imperial College Gliding Club
Lasham Airfield
Alton
Hampshire

Inkpen Gliding Club
Thruxton Airfield
Nr Andover
Hampshire

Lasham Gliding Society
Lasham Airfield
Nr Alton
Hampshire

Polish Air Force Gliding Association
Lasham Airfield
Nr Alton
Hampshire

Portsmouth Naval Gliding Club
RNAS Daedalus
Lee on Solent
Hampshire

Royal Aircraft Establishment Gliding
   Club
RAF Farnborough
Hampshire

Scout Association Gliding Club
Lasham Airfield
Nr Alton
Hampshire

Southdown Gliding Club
Parham
Nr Storrington
West Sussex

South Wales Gliding Club
1 Larch Grove
Lisvane
Cardiff

Surrey & Hants Gliding Club
Lasham Airfield
Nr Alton
Hampshire

Swindon Gliding Club
South Marston Airfield
Swindon
Wiltshire

Vectis Gliding Club
Sandown Airport
Sandown
Isle of Wight

West Wales Gliding Association
Withybush Airfield
Haverfordwest
Pembrokeshire

Woodspring Gliding Club
Western Super Mare Airfield
Western Super Mare
Avon

Midlands

Aquilla Gliding Club
13 Fallowfields
Bicester
Oxfordshire

Bristol & Gloucestershire Gliding Club
Nympsfield
Nr Stonehouse
Gloucestershire

Buckminister Gliding Club
Saltby Airfield
Saltby
Leicestershire

Cambridgeshire University Gliding Club
Cambridge Airport
Newmarket Road
Cambridge

Cotswold Gliding Club
Aston Down Airfield
Nr Minchampton
Gloucestershire

Coventry Gliding Club
Husbands Bosworth Airfield
Lutterworth
Leicestershire

Cranfield Institute of Technology Gliding
   Club
Cranfield
Bedfordshire

Defford Aero Club
RRE Air Station Pershore
Pershore
Worcestershire

Enstone Eagles Gliding Club
Enstone Airfield
Chipping Norton
Oxfordshire

Essex & Suffolk Gliding Club
Barrads Hall Airstrip
Whatfield
Hadleigh
Suffolk

Herefordshire Gliding Club
Shobden Airfield
Leominster
Herefordshire

Midland Gliding Club
The Long Mynd
Church Stretton
Shropshire

Norfolk Gliding Club
Tibenham Airfield
Nr Norwich
Norfolk

Norwich Soaring Group
RAF Swanton Morley
East Dereham
Norfolk

Oxford Gliding Club
RAF Western On The Green
Bicester
Oxfordshire

Peterborough & Spalding Gliding Club
Crowland Airfield
Nr Peterborough

Rattlesdon Gliding Club
Castle Lodge
Felsham
Bury St Edmunds
Suffolk

South Yorkshire Gliding Club
Winthorpe Airfield
Nr Newark
Nottinghamshire

Staffordshire Gliding Club
Morridge
Nr Leek
Staffordshire

Stratford upon Avon Gliding Club
Long Marston Airfield
Nr Stratford upon Avon
Warwickshire

Trent Valley Gliding Club
Kirton in Lindsey
Nr Gainsborough
Lincolnshire

Upward Bound Trust Gliding Club
Thame Airfield
Haddenham
Buckinghamshire

Weeland Gliding Club
Marshalls Farm
Careby
Stamford Lincolnshire

The North

Blackpool & Fylde Gliding Club
Cock Hill Farm
Fiddlers Lane
Chipping
Nr Preston
Lancashire

The Borders Gliding Club
Millfield Aerodrome
Nr Wooler
Northumberland

Burton & Derby Gliding Club
Church Broughton Airfield
Uttoxeter Road
Fosten
Derbyshire

Derby & Lancs Gliding Club
Camphill
Great Hucklow
Tideswell
Derbyshire

Doncaster & District Gliding Club
The Airport
Ellers Road
Besscarr
Doncaster
South Yorkshire

Hambletons Gliding Club
RAF Dishforth
Boroughbridge
Yorkshire

Lakes Gliding Club
Walney Airfield
Barrow in Furness
Lancashire

Newcastle & Teeside Gliding Club
Carlton Moor
Carlton in Cleveland
Middlesborough

Northumbria Gliding Club
Currock Hill
Chopwell
Newcastle on Tyne

Ouse Gliding Club
RAF Rufforth
Yorkshire

Tyne & Wear Gliding Club
Sunderland Airport
Washington Road
Sunderland
Tyne & Wear

Wolds Gliding Club
The Airfield
Pocklington
Yorkshire

Yorkshire Gliding Club
Sutton Bank
Thirsk
Yorkshire

Scotland

Angus Gliding Club
Condor
Angus
Arbroath

Cairngorm Gliding Club
Feshie Airstrip
Blackmill Farm
Kincraig
Invernesshire

Deeside Gliding Club
Aboyne Airfield
Dinnet
Aberdeenshire

Dumfries & District Gliding Club
Falgunzeon
Dalbeattie
Kirkudbrightshire

Glasgow & West of Scotland
  Gliding Club
Portmoak Airfield
Kinross
Kinrosshire

Highland Gliding Club
Milltown Airfield
Elgin
Morayshire

Islay Gliding Club
Port Ellen Aerodrome
Isle of Islay

Kirknewtown Gliding Club
Portmoak Airfield
Kinross
Kinrosshire

Lanarkshire Gliding Club
Strathaven Airfield
Strathaven
Lanarkshire

Scottish Gliding Union
Portmoak Airfield
Kinross
Kinrosshire

University of Glasgow & Strathclyde
  Gliding Club
Couplwa Farm
Nr Strathaven
Lanarkshire

Northern Ireland

Ulster Gliding Club
Newtownards Airfield
Newtownards Co Down

The prone position.

4   Where to hang glide

Airsports
Cwn Rheidol
Aberystwyth
Dyfed

Baileys Yorkshire Hang Gliding &
    Microlight Centre
2 Denton Avenue
Leeds

Cairnwell Hang Gliding
Cairnwell Mountain
By Braemar
Aberdeenshire

Devon School of Hang Gliding
1 Dovedale Road
Beacon Park
Plymouth
Devon

Free Flight Hang Gliding School
135 Sunningdale Avenue
Biggin Hill
Kent

Hampshire Flight Training Centre
21 Penns Road
Petersfield
Hants

Hungerford Hang Gliding Centre
The Bungalow
Wolf Hall Manor
Burbage
Marlborough
Wilts

Isle of Wight Hang Gliding Club &
    Training Centre
Rose Cottage
Clay Lane
Newbridge
Isle of Wight

Kent Hang Gliding School
Robus House
Silverland Road
Lyminge
Kent

Mercian Hang Gliding School
40 Moseley Road
Kenilworth
Warwickshire

Northern Hang Gliding Centre
Staxton
Nr Scarborough
North Yorkshire

Northern School of Hang Gliding
8 Brencon Avenue
Brooklands
Manchester

Northern School of Hang Gliding
52 Crescent Road
Sheffield

Peak Hang Gliding School Ltd
Macclesfield Road
Leek
Staffordshire

Peak School of Hang Gliding
65c Berry Hedge Lane
Winshill
Burton on Trent
Staffordshire

Peninsula Flight Ltd
South West Hang Gliding Centre
2 Neath Road
St Judes
Plymouth
Devon

Skyriders British Hang Gliders &
  Microlight Flying School
15 St Marys Green
Biggin Hill
Kent

Skysports British Hang Gliding
  Abergavenny
Head Office
Skysports Surrey
Lightwater
Surrey

Sussex College of Hang Gliding
18b Queens Road
Brighton
Sussex

Ultra Sports
Truleigh Sands Buildings
Truleigh Farm
Edburton
Nr Henfield
Sussex

Welsh Hang Gliding Centre
16 New Road
Crickhowell
Powys
South Wales

5 Where to microlight

Airborne
3 Woodlinken Close
Verwood
Dorset

Airsports
Cwm Rheidol
Aberystwyth
Dyfed

Birdman Flight Training
Mildenhall
Marlborough
Wiltshire

Blois Aviation
Cockfield Hall
Yoxford
Saxmundham
Suffolk

Breen Aviation
Enstone Airfield
Oxfordshire

The East Anglian Microlight Centre
1 St Peter's Road
Wisbech
Cambridgeshire

Flylight Southeast
Lydd Airport
Romney Marsh
Kent

Headcorn Microlight Club
Headcorn Airfield
Nr Ashford
Kent

Inkerman Air Services
26 High Street
Bramley
Guildford

Kent Microlight Aviation Centre
124 Punch Croft
New Ash Green
Kent

Long Marston Aviation Club
The Control Tower
Long Marston Airfield
Stratford upon Avon

Micro Aviation Ltd
Halfpenny Green Airport
Bobbington
West Midlands

Osprey Aviation
Sherwood
Lower Seagry
Chippenham
Wiltshire

Pegasus Ltd
21-24 Queen's Chambers
King Street
Nottingham

Skyhook Sailwings Ltd
Vale Mill
Chamber Road
Hollinwood
Oldham
Lancs

South West Airsports Ltd
Barton
Bolventnor
Launceston
Cornwall

Wind Sport Centre
The Control Tower
Kirbymoreside
York

---

6 Where to balloon

Anglia Balloons Ltd
Glenn Barrett
4 Howard Mews
Norwich

Balloon Stable Ltd
12 Burdett Street
Ramsbury
Wiltshire

Cirrus Balloon School
Saffords Farm
Fressingfield
Suffolk

Philip Clark
88 Greville Road
Bristol

Dr I Jacobs
Flat 3
23 Arkwright Road
London

Peter Langford
7 Glencairn Drive
London

Nottingham & Sheffield Hot Air Balloon
   Club
Pat Toll
5/13 Upper Parliament Street
Nottingham

Dave Partridge
15 Caledonia Place
Clifton
Bristol

Skysales Ltd
249 Passage Road
Bristol

Nigel Tasker
3 Montague Place
Bristol

Thunder Balloons Ltd
75 Leonard Street
London

---

7 Where to parachute

Full time

Ashford Parachute Centre
Ashford Airport
Lympne
Kent

British Parachute Schools
Langer Airfield
Langer
Nottinghamshire

British Skysports
Bridlington Aerodrome
Bridlington
Yorkshire

Cornwall Parachute Centre
Frans Ranch
Wadebridge
Cornwall

Fashions in balloons. Any number of colours and patterns can be made to suit the balloonist's requirements.

East Coast Parachute Centre
West Road
Clacton on Sea
Essex

Headcorn Parachute Club
Headcorn Airfield
Headcorn
Kent

Hereford Parachute Centre
Shobden Aerodrome
Leominster
Hereford

Ipswich Parachute Centre
Ipswich Airport
Nacton Road
Ipswich

Lincoln Parachute Centre
Sturgate Aerodrome
Upton
Nr Gainsborough
Lincolnshire

Montford Bridge Para Centre
The Airfield
Montford Bridge
Shrewsbury

Peterborough Parachute Centre
Sibson Airfield
Wansford
Peterborough
Cambridgeshire

RSA Parachute Club
Thruxton Aerodrome
Andover
Hampshire

Weekend-only clubs

Black Knights Parachute Centre
Pattys Farm
Cockerham
Nr Lancaster

Cambridge University Free Fall Club
30 Green End Road
Cambridge

Duck End Parachute Group
Rectory Farm
Abbotsley
Huntingdon
Cambridgeshire

The Glenrothers School of Parachuting
Glenrothes
Fife

Halfpenny Green Skydiving Club
Bobbington
Nr Stourbridge
West Midlands

Leeds/Bradford Free Fall Club
Elvington Airfield
Yorks

Manchester Free Fall Club
Tilstock DZ
Twemlows Hall Farm
Whitchurch
Shropshire

Martlesham Heath Para Club
Flixton Airfield
Bungay
Suffolk

Midland Parachute Centre
Long Marston Airfield
Nr Stratford upon Avon
Warwickshire

North West Para Centre
Cark Airfield
Flockborough
Nr Grange over Sands
Lancashire

Scottish Parachute Club
Strathalan Castle
Auchterarder
Perthshire

South Cotswold Parachute Club
Badminton
Avon

Sunderland Parachute Centre
Sunderland Airport
Sunderland
Tyne & Wear

TAS School of Parachuting
Tilstock Airfield
Whitchurch
Shropshire

TPA Parachute Centre
Elvington Airfield
Nr York

West Lancs Parachute Centre
Burscough Airfield
Nr Ormskirk
Lancashire

8   Useful addresses

Aircraft Owners and Pilots Association
50a Cambridge Street
London

British Aerobatic Association
62 Ennerdale Road
Kew
Richmond
Surrey

British Balloon and Airship Club
Kimberly House
Vaughn Way
Leicester

British Gliding Association
Kimberly House
Vaughn Way
Leicester

British Hang Gliding Association
Monksilver
Taunton
Somerset

British Helicopter Advisory Board
Knowles House
Cromwell Road
Redhill
Surrey

British Microlight
Aircraft Association
Membership Dept, E7 Stafford
Park 4, Telford
Shropshire

British Parachute Association
Kimberly House
Vaughn Way
Leicester

Formula 1 Air Racing Association
50a Cambridge Street
London

Man Powered Aircraft Group
Royal Aeronautical Society
4 Hamilton Place
London

Popular Flying Association
Terminal Building
Shoreham Airport
Shoreham
Sussex

United States Hang Gliding
  Association Inc
Box 66306
Los Angeles
California 90066
USA

9   Overseas flying training organisations

Airspace International Ltd
Alderney House
58 Normandy Street
Alton
Hants

American Flight Centre Inc.
3900 N Main Building
2 - S
Fort Worth
Texas 76106
USA

American Flyers
DuPage Airport
West Chicago
Illinois 60185
USA

Anglo American International
Flight Academy
Meecham Field
Fort Worth
Texas 76106
 USA

AVIA Corporation
1951 Airport Road
Atlanta
Georgia
USA

Aviation Training Inc
21593 Skywest Drive
Hayward
California 94541
USA

Brantly Hynes Helicopters
PO Box 697
Frederick
Oklahoma
USA

Burnside Ott
Aviation Training Centre
Building 106
Opa—Locka Airport
Miami
Florida 33054
USA

Carib Helicopters Inc
14250 S W 129th St
Miami
Florida 33186
USA

Curzon Flight
The Old Barn House
High Road
Eastcote
Pinner
Middlesex
UK

Emery School of Aviation
Dept H
661 Buss Avenue
Greeley
Colorado 80631
USA

Flight Proficiency Inc
PO Box 7510
Dept E
Dallas
Texas 75209
USA

HAL Aviation
1701E 5th Street
Kennett
Missouri 63857
USA

Island Helicopter Corp
North Avenue
Garden City
New York 11530
USA

Kingston Air Services
Flight Training Centre
Normon Rogers Airport
Kingston
Ontario
Canada

Mercury Flight Services
23000 Stuebmer Airline
Spring Houston
Texas 77379
USA

Omniflight Helicopters
Route 7
Highway 51 South
Janesville
Wisconsin 53545
USA

Pacific Wing & Rotor Inc.
3605 E Spring Street
Suite 210
Long Beach
California 90806
USA

Pilot Personnel International
3520 Knox Bute Road
Albany
Oregon 97321
USA

Professional Aviation Inc.
923 West Deer Valley Road
Phoenix
Arizona 85027
USA

Ranger Helicopters Ltd
Sault Ste Maries
Ontario
Canada

A G Rotors Inc
Box 578
Dept FL Gettysburg
Pennsylvania 17325
USA

Sierra Academy of Aeronautics
Oakland International Airport
Oakland
California 94614
USA

Slaton Flying Service
PO Box 429
Slaton
Texas 79364
USA

Sowell Aviation Company
PO Box 1490
Municipal Airport
Panama City
Florida 32401
USA

Tacata Airways Ltd
Box 1328
Uxbridge
Ontario
Canada

Western Aviation Flight Center
2655 Robert Fowler Way
San Jose
California 95148
USA

Western Hills Aviation Inc
3816 Fort Worth HWY
Weatherford
Texas 76986
USA

Wondel Aviation Ltd
6200 Airport Road
St-Hubert
Quebec J3Y 5K2
Canada

10   Suggested books for further reading

Light aircraft

Airborne For Pleasure, Albert Morgan.
Flying Facts, David Ogilvy.
Private Pilot Studies, S.E.T. Taylor &
   H.A. Parmer.
Your Private Pilot's Licence, Betty Cones.
Pilots Manual, J.S. Evans.
Flight Briefing For Pilots (Vols 1-6),
   Neville Birch & Alan Bramson.
Flying Start, Mary Francis.
Cleared For Take Off, Gordon Stokes.
Aerobatics, Neil Williams.
Aeromedicine For Aviators, Keith Reid.
Aviation Law For Pilots, S.E.T. Taylor &
   H.A. Parmer.
Be A Better Pilot, Alan Bramson.
Build and Fly Your Own Plane,
   Robert Lowe.
Flight Safety Aerodynamics, Aage Roed.
Flight Safety, Richard Collins.
Fly On Instruments, George C. Larson.
Ground Studies For Pilots (Vols 1-3),
   S.E.T. Taylor & H.A. Parmer.
Instrument Flying, R.L. Taylor.
Light Aircraft Inspection, J.E. Heywood.
R/T Exam For The PPL,
   Geoffrey Dunster.
The Technical Exam For The PPL,
   Geoffrey Dunster.
The Instrument Rating, Neville Birch.
Using An Aircraft Radio, C.L. Day.
Weather Flying, Robert Buck.

Magazines

Flight International
Quadrant House
The Quadrant
Sutton
Surey
SM2 5AS

Flying Magazine
One Park Avenue
New York
New York 10016
USA

Pilot Magazine
88 Burlington Road
New Malden
Surrey
KT3 4NT

Popular Flying
Terminal Building
Shoreham Airport
Shoreham
Sussex

Helicopters

The Helicopter, John Fay.
Airborne For Pleasure, Albert Morgan.
Helicopter Design & Data Manual,
   S.J. Dzik.
All About Helicopters, John Howard.
Helicopters Of The World, John Taylor.
Guide To Rotorcraft, David Thomas.
Basic Helicopter Handbook, Federal
   Aviation Administration.

Magazines

Helicopter International
Delta House
Summer Lane
Worle
Weston-super-Mare
Avon
BS22 0BE

Rotor & Wing International
PJS Publications
News Plaza
Box 1790
Peoria
Illinois 61656
USA

Gliding

New Soaring Pilot, Ann & Lorne Welch.
Beginning Gliding, Derek Piggott.
Airborne For Pleasure, Albert Morgan.
Airsports, Ann Welch.
The Story Of Gliding, Ann Welch.
Gliding & Soaring, Bill Scull.
Gliding, Derek Piggott.
On Being A Bird, Phillip Wills.
Glider Pilot, Peter Champion.
Going Solo, Derek Piggott.
Accidents Happen, Ann Welch.
Elementary Gliding, Paul Blanchard.
Flying Training In Gliders, Ann Welch.
Gliding Competitively, John Delafield.
Janes World Sailplanes, Andrew Coates.
Meteorology For Glider Pilots,
   C.E. Wallington.
Principles Of Flight, Bill Scull.
Understanding Gliding, Derek Piggott.
Theory Of Flight For Glider Pilots,
   Ray Stafford Allen.
Soaring Across Country, Bill Scull.
Flying Sailplanes, Helmut Reichmann.
The Weather Guide, A.G. Forsdyke.

Magazines

Australian Gliding Monthly
Box 1650
GPO
Adelaide
South Australia
5001

Gliding Kiwi
Private Bag
Tauranga
New Zealand

Sailplane & Gliding
British Gliding Association
Kimberly House
Vaughn Way
Leicester

Soaring Magazine
Box 66071
Los Angeles
California 90066
USA

Hang gliding and microlights

Airsports, Ann Welch.
Hang Glider Pilot, Ann Welch &
   Gerry Breen.
Airborne For Pleasure, Albert Morgan.
An Introduction To Hang Gliding,
   Bob Mackay.
Soaring Hang Gliders, Ann Welch
   & Roy Hill.
Hang Gliding Don'ts and Don'ts,
   Bob Mackay.
Air Medical Notes For Hang Glider Pilots,
   Dunstan Hadley.
Know The Game—Hang Gliding,
   Ann Welch.

Magazines

Flight Line Magazine
British Microlight Aircraft Association
Membership Dept
E7 Stafford Park 4
Telford
Shropshire
TF3 3BA

Wings Magazine
British Hang Gliding Association
Monksilver
Taunton
Somerset

Ballooning

Airsports, Ann Welch.
Hot Air Ballooning, Christine Turnbull.
Ballooning, Dick Wirth & Jerry Young.
Airships: An Illustrated History,
   Henry Beaubois & Carlo Demand.

Airships For The Future, William J. White.
Back To The Drawing Board,
   Allen Andrews.
Balloons, Charles Dollfus.
Balloons & Airships, Lennart Ege.
The Balloon Book, Paul Fillingham.
The Blimp Book, George Hall &
   George Larson.
The Book Of Balloons, Erik Norgaard.
The Dangerous Sort, Anthony Smith.
Five Weeks In A Balloon, Jules Verne.
Riders Of The Winds, Don Dwiggins.
Airborne For Pleasure, Albert Morgan.

Magazines

Aerostat
Kimberly House
Vaughn Way
Leicester

Ballooning Journal
2226 Beebee Street
San Luis Obispo
California 93401
USA

Parachuting

Airsports, Ann Welch.
Airborne For Pleasure, Albert Morgan.
The Art Of Freefall Relative Work,
   Pat Works.
The Parachute Manual, Dan Poynter.
Parachuting, Dan Poynter.
Skies Call, Andy Keech.
The Falcons Disciples, Howard Gregory.
Falling Free, Cathy Williamson.
Parachuting & Skydiving,
   Dumbo Williams.
Panic Takes Time, Dumbo Williams.
Sport Parachuting, Russ Gunby.
The Space Age Sport, Ray Derby.
Sport Parachuting, Charles-Shea Simonds.
Parachutist, Peter Hearn.
Alone In The Sky, Mike Reilly.
Parachuting For Sport, Jim Greenwood.
Birdman, Leo Valentine.
Skydiving, Bud Sellick.

Magazines

Parachutist Magazine
806 15th Street NW
Suite 444
Washington DC 20005
USA

Sport Parachutist
Kimberly House
Vaughn Way
Leicester

11 Key to abbreviations and terms

The following abbreviations do not necessarily pertain to the chapters in this book but may be useful to the reader.

AD Airworthiness directive, issued by the authorities to correct a defect found in an aircraft type after certification.

ADF Automatic direction finder, a radio compass which gives a relative bearing to the radio station to which it is tuned.

ADIZ Air defence identification zone. A block of airspace extending upwards from the surface of the ground or sea within which ready identification, location and the control of aircraft are required in the interests of national security.

Advancing blade That half of the rotor disc in which the rotation of the blade is moving in the same direction as the movement of the helicopter. If the helicopter is moving forward the advancing blade will be in the right half of the rotor disc, if moving backward it will be in the left half. If moving sideward to the left it will be in the forward half and if moving sideward to the right it will be in the rear half.

AFI Assistant flying instructor.

AGL Above ground level.

AIB Accident Investigation Branch of the Department of Trade.

AIC Aeronautical information circular.

Ailerons Moveable control surfaces at the trailing edges of the wings. Primary effect is roll about the longitudinal axis of the aircraft.

Airfoil Any surface designed to obtain a useful reaction from the air through which it moves in the form of lift.

Airspeed Speed of an aircraft in relation to the relative airflow.

Airspeed indicator Instrument which shows the airspeed.

Alternate An airfield detailed in the flight plan to which the aeroplane will proceed if a landing at the intended destination is not possible.

Altimeter Pressure operated instrument recording height above sea level or above ground according to setting.

Altitude Height above sea level.

AMSL Above mean sea level.

Angle of attack The angle between the cord line of the wing and the airflow. The angle at which the air flow strikes the wing.

ANO Air navigation order, the legal instrument defining air law, navigation

and licence issue in the United Kingdom.

AOA Aerodrome Owners' Association.

AOC Air operator's certificate. Issued by the Civil Aviation Authority and required by aircraft operators flying charter or scheduled public service flights.

AOG Aircraft on ground. A term used to denote urgency when requesting aircraft spare parts from the manufacturers or suppliers, meaning that the aircraft cannot fly until the replacement parts have been delivered.

AOPA Aircraft Owners' and Pilots' Association.

APU Auxiliary power unit. Jet aircraft have auxiliary power units to provide power for engine starting and for running the aircraft's systems when on the ground.

ARB Airworthiness Requirements Board for the CAA which issues airworthiness certificates for aircraft.

Articulated rotor A rotor system in which the blades are free to flap, drag and feather.

Aspect ratio The ratio of wingspan to width of the wing.

ATC Air traffic control.

ATCO Air traffic control officer.

ATIS Automatic terminal information service a continuous recorded broadcast of routine airport information.

ATOA Air Taxi Operators' Association.

ATPL Airline transport pilot's licence.

ATZ Aerodrome traffic zone. A region of protected airspace surrounding an airfield which has a horizontal radius of 1.5 nautical miles from the airfield boundary extending up to 600 m (2,000 ft) above the airfield elevation.

AUW All up weight, a term for the total loaded weight of an aircraft. Maximum auw is the maximum allowable weight, including payload and fuel specified in the aircraft's certificate of airworthiness.

Back course Some of the localiser transmitters used in instrument landing systems radiate a back beam in the opposite direction to the approach for which the aid is intended.

BAeA British Aerobatic Association.

BALPA British Airline Pilots' Association.

BAUA Business Aircraft Users' Association.
BGA British Gliding Association.
BGHA British Hang Gliding Association.
BHAB British Helicopter Advisory Board.
Billow The fullness of each half of a Rogallo sail when inflated in flight.
Blade damper A device spring, friction or hydraulic installed on the vertical drag hinge to diminish or dampen blade oscillation hunting around this hinge.
Blade loading The loads placed on the rotor blades of a helicopter, determined by dividing the gross weight of the helicopter by the combined area of all the rotor blades.
BMAA British Microlight Aircraft Association.

CAP Civil air publications, information issued by the CAA i.e. CAP 53 *The private pilot licence.*
CAT Clean air turbulence.
CAVOK Pronounced CAV-OK. Used in weather conditions of at least ten kilometres (six miles) visibility with no cloud below 1,525 m (5,000 ft).
CAVU Ceiling and visibility unlimited—cloudless conditions with visibility in excess of ten kilometers (six miles).
CDI Course deviation indicator, the vertical needle of a VOR which shows the aircraft's position relative to the selected VOR radial.
Ceiling The height above ground or water of the base of the lowest layer of cloud.
Centre of Gravity Point about which an aircraft would balance exactly.
Centre of pressure The imaginary point on the chord line where the resultant of all aerodynamic forces of an airfoil section may be considered to be concentrated.
Centrifugal force The force created by the tendency of a body to follow a straight line path against the force which causes it to move in a curve, resulting in a force which tends to pull away from the axis of rotation.
CFI Chief flying instructor.
Chord The width of the wing measured from the leading edge to the trailing edge.
Circuit An imaginary pattern flown around an aerodrome.
Collective pitch control The method of control by which the pitch of all rotor blades is varied equally and simultaneously.
Coriolis effect The tendency of a mass to increase or decrease its angular velocity when its radius of rotation is increased or decreased respectively.
Course The intended direction of flight.
CPL Commercial Pilot's licence.
CRT Cathode ray tube about to be used in aircraft cockpits in place of conventional instruments.
CS Constant speed, a controllable pitch propeller which maintains constant rpm by altering the angle of the propeller blades automatically in relation to the power setting of the engine.
CVR Cockpit voice recorder.
Cyclic pitch control The control which changes the pitch of the rotor blades individually during a cycle of revolution to control the tilt of the rotor disc and therefore the direction and velocity of horizontal flight.

D & D Distress and diversion cell at the London air traffic control centre providing 24-hour watch on emergency radio frequencies who can locate and help pilots who are lost or have some other inflight emergency.
Delta Hinge The hinge with its axis parallel to the rotor plane of rotation which permits the rotor blades to flap to equalise lift between the advancing half and the retreating half of the rotor disc.
Delta sailwing Any flexible wing hang glider of delta or triangular shape.
Density altitude Pressure altitude corrected for temperature and humidity.
DF Direction finding, a DF steer can be provided by aerodromes having direction finding equipment which locates an aircraft and gives it a vector to steer to the aerodrome.
DH Decision height, the altitude at which a pilot making an ils approach decides to continue with the approach or go around.
Direction indicator Gyroscopic instrument which when set to the compass will show the direction the aircraft is pointing.
Disc area The area swept by the blades of the rotor. This is a circle with its centre at the hub axis and a radius of one blade length.
Disc loading The ratio of the helicopter gross weight to rotor disc area (total helicopter weight divided by the rotor disc area).
Dissymmetry of lift The unequal lift across the rotor disc resulting from the difference in the velocity of air over the

advancing blade half and the retreating blade half of the rotor disc area.

DME Distance measuring equipment, a combination of ground and airborne equipment which gives a continuous distance from station readout by measuring the time lapse of a signal from the aircraft to the ground station and back.

Doppler Doppler effect is the change in frequency in light, sound or radio waves when source and receiver are in relative motion. Doppler radar systems use this effect for navigation.

Drift Deviation from intended track.

EAA Experimental Aircraft Association.

EAT Estimated approach time.

EGT Exhaust gas temperature a cockpit device which gives the pilot a read out of the exhaust gas temperature of an aero engine.

ELT Emergency locator transmitter. An ELT transmitter is a small radio beacon fixed to the aircraft which is automatically activated by impact or immersion in water and transmits a continuous tone on emergency radio frequencies helping rescue helicopters or search parties locate the crash site.

ETA Estimated time of arrival.

ETD Estimated time of departure.

ETE Estimated time en route.

FAA Federal Aviation Administration.

FAF Final approach fix, the point at which an instrument approach begins.

FAI Federation Aeronautique Internationale, the international body for the verification of aeronautical records and regulations.

FBO Fixed base operator.

Feathering action The action which changes the pitch angle of the rotor blades periodically by rotating them around their axis.

Feathering axis The axis about which the pitch angle of a rotor blade is varied. Sometimes referred to as the spanwise axis.

FIN Vertical section of an aircraft tail unit.

Finals The part of a landing sequence or circuit procedure in which the aircraft has made its final turn and is inbound to the duty runway.

FIR Flight information region. United Kingdom airspace is divided into two regions, London and Scottish, throughout which pilots can get a number of services and information from the appropriate air traffic control centre.

FL Flight level. A level of constant atmospheric pressure at which an aircraft with its altimeter set to a standard pressure of 1013.2 millibars will fly expressed in round metres (hundreds of feet).

Flapping The vertical movement of a blade about a delta (flapping) hinge.

Flaps Moveable sections at trailing edges of wings which can be lowered to increase lift.

Flare out or flare The change from a steady descent to level flight just above the ground prior to landing.

FOB Fuel on board.

FPM Feet per minute.

Freewheeling unit A component part of the transmission or power train which automatically disconnects the main rotor from the engine when the engine stops or slows below the equivalent of rotor rpm.

Fuselage Section of an aircraft excluding wings and tail unit, housing pilot, passengers, controls and engine.

G The acceleration force of gravity.

GA General aviation. All flying not covered by military or airline operations.

GADO General Aviation District Office.

GAMA General Aviation Manufacturers' Association.

GAMTA General Aviation Manufacturers' and Traders' Association.

GCA Ground controlled approach. A ground controller gives verbal descent guidance to the pilot using a precision radar to monitor his approach path.

GFT General flying test. The flying test taken by all student pilots before qualifying for their private pilot's licence.

Glide ratio The ratio between the distance flown and the height lost of a glider in flight, e.g., glide ratio 5 to 1 means that the glider will fly a theoretical distance of 500 m from an altitude of 100 m.

GMT Greenwich mean time.

GNAV Graphic area navigation. A system of direct point-to-point navigation using a VOR/DME and special printed charts.

GPWS Ground proximity warning system. A radar based device which gives pilots an audible warning of terrain close to an aeroplane's flight path.

Ground effect The cushion of denser air confined beneath the rotor system of a hovering helicopter which gives additional lift and thus decreases the power required to hover.

Groundspeed Actual speed of aircraft relative to the ground beneath it.
GS Glide slope. The vertical part of a guidance instrument landing system which gives a safe glide path to the runway.
Gyroscopic precession A characteristic of all rotating bodies. When a force is applied to the periphery of a rotating body parallel to its axis of rotation, the body will tilt in the direction of the applied force 90 degrees later in the plane of rotation.

HAI Helicopter Association International.
Heading Direction in which the aircraft is pointing.
HF High frequency radio band used for long range communications in the 3.30 Mhz range.
Holding pattern A racetrack manoeuvre to keep an aircraft within specified airspace while awaiting further instructions from air traffic control.
Hovering in ground effect Maintaining a fixed position over a spot on the ground or water which compresses a cushion of high density air between the main rotor and the ground or water surface and thus increases the lift produced by the main rotor. Normally the main rotor must be within one half rotor diameter to the ground or water surface in order to produce an efficient ground effect.
Hovering out of ground effect Maintaining a fixed position over a spot on the ground or water at some altitude above the ground at which no additional lift is obtained from the ground effect.
HSI Horizontal situation indicator. A cockpit navigation display often part of a flight director system.
HUD Head up display. A system of projecting information visually on to the windscreen of a military fighter aircraft.
Hunting The tendency of a blade (due to coriolis effect) to seek a position ahead of or behind that which would be determined by centrifugal force alone.

IAS Indicated air speed.
IATA International Air Transport Association.
ICAO International Civil Aviation Organisation.
IF Instrument flying.
IFR Instrument flight rules.
ILS Instrument landing system is the standard bad weather landing aid which uses radio beams to provide the pilot with vertical and horizontal guidance during the approach to land. The localiser gives azimuth guidance while the glide slope defines the correct descent profile. Marker beacons and high intensity runway lights are also part of the ILS system. Indicators in the cockpit take the form of needles, bars or LEDs.
IMC Instrument meteorological conditions. Weather conditions below the VMC mins.
INS Inertial navigation system. A gyroscopic based instrument which senses acceleration deceleration and directional change thus computing the aircrafts position with great accuracy. Mostly used in jet aircraft and some business aeroplanes.
ISA International standard atmosphere. A set of standard conditions of temperature and pressure which serve as a basis for comparing actual conditions.
Isobars Lines drawn on weather maps joining points of equal pressure.

KHz Kilohertz. The frequency of a radio wave measured in thousands of cycles per second.
Knot One nautical mile per hour. The standard unit of speed measurement in aviation.

LATCC London Air Traffic Control Centre.
LF Low frequency.
Locator A low medium frequency non directional beacon used as an aid during an aircraft's final approach.
Loran A low frequency over ocean radio navigation system.
LTA Lighter than air.

Mach The ratio of true airspeed to the speed of sound Mach 1 being the speed of sound.
Matz Military air traffic zone. An area of protected airspace around certain military airfields normally extending for an 8 km (5 mile) radius around the airfield and from the ground level to 915 m (3,000 ft) above aerodrome level.
Mayday International radio distress call.
MEA Minimum en route altitude.
MHz Megahertz. The frequency of radio waves measured in millions of cycles per second.
Minimums Weather condition requirements for a particular mode of flight.
Mixture control Enables the pilot to vary

the mixture of petrol and air going to the engine.

MLS Microwave landing system. A microwave based instrument landing and approach system which is replacing the ILS system.

NATS National Air Traffic Services. A part of the CAA which provides air traffic control in the UK.

NBAA National Business Aircraft Association.

NDB Non directional beacon. A medium frequency aid which transmits non directional signals with a morse code identifier superimposed on the signal. Signals are received by the aircrafts ADF.

NOTAM Notices to airmen issued by the CAA to notify pilots of new or changed aeronautical facilities or hazards.

NTSB National Transportation Safety Board.

OASC Officer and aircrew selection centre. The facility at RAF Biggin Hill in Kent where aircrew candidates for the Army Air Corps, Marines, Fleet Air Arm and Royal Air Force are selected.

OAT Outside air temperature.

OBS Omni bearing selector is part of a VOR indicator and is the knob used to select a radial from a VOR.

Overshoot To climb away from a runway after making an approach to land.

PAN International radio call signifying urgency.

PAPI Precision approach path indicator.

PAR Precision approach radar providing an air traffic controller with information on range, altitude and heading of an aircraft on final approach enabling him to talk down a pilot in instrument conditions.

PFA Popular Flying Association.

Phonetic alphabet

A	Alpha	N	November
B	Bravo	O	Oscar
C	Charlie	P	Papa
D	Delta	Q	Quebec
E	Echo	R	Romeo
F	Foxtrot	S	Sierra
G	Golf	T	Tango
H	Hotel	U	Uniform
I	India	V	Victor
J	Juliet	W	Whisky
K	Kilo	X	X-ray
L	Lima	Y	Yankee
M	Mike	Z	Zulu

Pitch Movement about transverse axis—nose up or nose down.

Pitch angle The angle between the chord line of the rotor blade and the reference plane of the main rotor hub or the rotor plane of rotation.

Polar A diagrammatic presentation of performance giving rate of sink against airspeed.

PPL Private Pilot's licence.

PPO Prior permission only.

Procedure turn A manoeuvre which reverses the direction of an aircraft's flight in order to establish it on the intermediate or final approach course. The outbound course and distance in which the turn must be completed are specified in the published approach procedure.

PSI Pounds per square inch. A measure of pressure.

Q-code A code system developed in the days when air to ground communication was by morse transmission where many routine phrases and questions were reduced to three letters.

QDM The magnetic bearing of the direction finding station giving the bearing.

QFE Atmospheric pressure at aerodrome elevation. With its sub-scale set to the aerodrome QFE an altimeter will indicate height above that aerodrome.

QFI Qualified flying instructor.

QNH Altitude above mean sea level based on local station pressure.

RAS Rectified airspeed-indicated, airspeed corrected for instrument position error.

Reflex A reflex aerofoil is one in which the section curves slightly upwards towards the trailing edge. This improves the longitudinal (pitch) stability.

Required track Line drawn on map joining point of departure and destination.

Rigid rotor A rotor system with blades fixed to the hub in such a way that they can feather but cannot flap or drag.

RMI Radio magnetic indicator. A navigation aid consisting of a combined gyro compass VOR and or ADF display which will indicate aircraft heading, position relative to a selected VOR radial or bearing and with ADF the position of the aircraft's nose relative to the selected station.

RNAV Area navigation. A system of radio

navigation which gives point to point off airways navigation by displacement of VORs to any desired position via an onboard computer.

Rogallo Generic name for the delta shape hang glider originated by Francis Rogallo.

Roll Movement about longitudinal axis of aircraft.

RT Radio telephony.

Rudder Moveable section of trailing edge of fin used to help in steering.

RVR Runway visual range horizontal measurement of visibility along a runway.

SAR Search and rescue.

SAS Stability augmentation system. An automatic helicopter flight control system used to enhance handling qualities.

SATCO Senior air traffic control officer.

SBAC Society of British Aerospace Companies.

Semirigid rotor A rotor system in which the blades are fixed to the hub but are free to flap and feather.

SID Standard instrument departure. A standard IFR departure route which enables air traffic controllers to issue abbreviated clearances and thus speed the flow of IFR traffic.

SIGMET A warning of severe weather issued by meteorological offices.

Sink rate The rate of descent of a glider e.g. a sink speed of 3 m/sec. means that theoretically it will descend to earth at this rate.

Slip The controlled flight of a helicopter in a direction not in line with its fore and aft axis.

SOB Souls on board.

Socked in Airfield closed to traffic because of weather.

Solidity ratio The ratio of total rotor blade area to total rotor disc area.

SOP Standard operating procedure.

Spin State of autorotation aircraft descending nose steeply down.

Spoilers Any external surface which can be deflected into the airflow to create drag.

SRZ Special rules zone. An area of protected airspace surrounding an airfield extending from the surface upwards to a specific level which affords safety to air traffic movements in the vicinity of airfields whose traffic level does not warrant the setting up of a control zone.

SSR Secondary surveillance radar.

Stall Breakdown of airflow around wings.

Standard atmosphere Atmospheric conditions in which (1) the air is dry perfect gas, (2) the temperature at sea level is 59°F (15°C), (3) the pressure at sea level is 29.92 in of Hg and, (4) the temperature gradient is approximately 3.5°F (-15.8°C) per 30.5 m (1,000 ft) change in altitude.

STOL Short take off or landing.

TAF Terminal area forecast. A forecast of weather conditions expected at an aerodrome.

Tailplane Horizontal section of tail unit.

TAS True air speed is rectified airspeed corrected for height and outside air temperature.

Taxiing Movement of aircraft under power on the ground.

TBO Time between overhauls. The number of hours of operation that may be expected before an engine needs to be overhauled.

Tip draggers Spoilers usually vertical at the wingtips which can be deflected separately to create drag at one wingtip to cause the glider to yaw and turn.

Tip path plane The plane in which rotor blade tips travel when rotating.

Tip speed The rotative speed of the rotor at its blade tips.

Tip stall The stall condition on the retreating blade which occurs at high forward speeds.

TMA Terminal control area.

Torque A force or combination of forces that tends to produce a countering rotating motion. In a single rotor helicopter where the rotor turns counter-clockwise, the fuselage tends to rotate clockwise (looking down on the helicopter).

Track The flight path of an aircraft over the ground.

Translational lift The additional lift obtained through airspeed because of increased efficiency of the rotor system whether it be when transitioning from a hover into horizontal flight or when hovering in a wind.

Transponder The airborne receiver/transmitter part of the SSR system.

TSO Technical standard order.

Turnbuckles Another name for bottle-screws. Used to adjust the length of cables.

UAS University air squadron.

UHF Ultra high frequency radio frequencies in the 300-3,000 MHz band.

UIR Upper information region.
Undercarriage Wheels and their supporting legs.
U/S Unserviceable.

VASI Visual approach slope indicator. A coloured light system giving visual guidance to the glide path of a runway.
Venturi effect The speeding up of the air as it is drawn through a confined space.
VFR Visual flight rules.
VHF Very high frequency radio frequencies in the 30-300 MHz band used for most civil air ground communication.
VLF/OMEGA Worldwide system of long range area navigation.
VMC Visual meteorological conditions.
VOLMET Meteorological broadcasts of recorded weather at a selection of aerodromes.

VOR Very high frequency omnidirectional range. A radio navigational aid operating in the 108-118 MHz band. VOR is the most commonly used radio navigation aid in private flying but has limited range.
VP Variable pitch propeller.
VSI Vertical speed indicator. One of the primary flight instruments showing rate of climb and descent.

Yaw The skidding or sideways movement of an aircraft when it is not flying through the air in the direction it is pointing.

Zulu All times for flight operations anywhere in the world are given in zulu time, Greenwich Mean Time.